Navigating the Digital Sea offers readers a balanced approach that requires all of us to be both disciplined and deliberate while engaging in the dangers and hope of social media, challenging us to rely on the gospel as our guide for the glory of God.

—Bryant Lee, Senior Pastor,
Higher Expectations Church,
President of The Collaborative Fellowship

In a distracting culture of shallow universal connections and anemic relationships, Kort provides a helpful guide for leading a deep life and engaging in deep work. Highly recommend this timely book.

—Justin Hyde, Teaching Pastor,
Redeemer Church

We need a gospel response to the onslaught of media confronting our families today. Kort's book provides this response, guiding us to engage our culture with the gospel, as he encourages families to seek ways to redeem social media with wisdom and grace. This is a thoughtful, biblical, practical, and timely resource that exposes the dangers and opportunities of social media. Your eyes will be opened, and your heart, moved, leaving you resolved to swim these waters with a gospel stroke.

—Jonathan Williams, Author of *Gospel Family*
and Senior Pastor of Wilcrest Baptist Church,
Houston, Texas

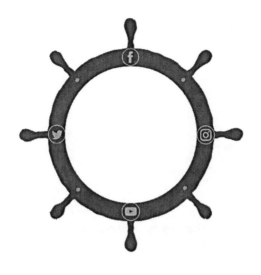

NAVIGATING
THE DIGITAL SEA

Gospel Guidance For Social Media

KORT MARLEY

LUCIDBOOKS

Navigating the Digital Sea: Gospel Guidance for Social Media
Copyright © 2016 by Kort Marley

Published by Lucid Books in Houston, TX.
www.LucidBooks.net

First Printing 2016

ISBN 10: 1632960982
ISBN 13: 9781632960986
eISBN 10: 1632960990
eISBN 13: 9781632960993

Special Sales: Most Lucid Books titles are available in special quantity discounts. Custom imprinting or excerpting can also be done to fit special needs. Contact Lucid Books at info@lucidbooks.net.

TABLE OF CONTENTS

INTRODUCTION:
CHARTING THE COURSE

Technology has changed the way we live. In a few short decades, the Internet has swept into our lives and claimed its place among the most significant cultural advancements the world has ever seen. And somehow social media is barely a decade old. In ten short years this new medium of communication has become a major part of most people's lives. It's hard to imagine a world now without hashtags, comment sections, and selfies.

I remember relaxing at my grandparents' house as a kid, watching *Lamb Chop's Play Along*, followed by *Mr. Rogers' Neighborhood*. My grandfather would amble in the room with a scowl on his face. Peering down at me, then back at the television, then back at me, he would say, "Boy, do you do anything except watch that idiot box?!"

I would respond to his question with a look of incredulity.

"Come on, Grandpa!"

His face was as unchanging as his opinion of my TV viewing habits.

"All that is, is pure poppycock, son."

Television was as ridiculous to him as I'm sure social

media is to many in my parents' generation. My grandfather's disapproval didn't sway me in the slightest, though. This was the beginning of my addiction.

In years to come, Homer Simpson entered my life as the bumbling father on *The Simpsons*; Danny Tanner sat me down for long talks alongside his daughter D.J. on *Full House*; Will Smith became personal aristocracy to me as *The Fresh Prince of Bel-Air*; and Steve Urkel became the nerd I hated to love on *Family Matters*. Later, I was introduced to ESPN's *Sportscenter* show where host Stuart Scott would feed me sports highlight after highlight before bed, which was "cooler than the other side of the pillow," as he often said.

Television was a big part of my life, and that is putting it mildly. I never questioned the craziness of it like my grandpa. It just *was*. It wasn't until an experience on a mission trip some years later that I was first awakened to TV's significant place in my daily life.

"Your people worship your screen boxes, no?" asked the translator. I looked at him with a puzzled expression. The local pastor and I had entered the home of a man who had asked for prayer. He had small, wooden figurines on his dresser and prominently displayed on his mantle. These were real, material, handcrafted idols, not the invisible heart idols more common in America.

The pastor had encouraged the man to purge his home of these idols before we prayed. I was struck by the insignificance of the figures, wondering how people could worship something so silly and trite. These wooden figures could never save, help, comfort, encourage, convict, judge, or restore anything or anyone!

The local pastor looked at me and asked, "Your people worship your screen boxes, no?"

The translator explained to me that he was referring to our television sets. I laughed. "No, no, no. This is nothing like that." The pastor looked puzzled.

"Then why does all your furniture face the screen box then?"

I was stunned. I had never considered it. In fact, I had never even noticed it. Every piece of furniture in my living room was strategically placed around the television set. Now, to be clear, this wasn't a conscious worship decision by me. Yet, to this pastor in a village that had no access to such technology, it was a worship decision all the way. Perhaps his understanding of worship was far wiser than I understood at the time.

Television had taken its place in our homes the same way it had taken its place in our lives—without us considering it too deeply. Before we knew it, it just was a part of life. But to people like my grandfather and the local pastor of that village, it was easy to see the pervasive nature of TV viewing in the lives of so many. We were unaware of something so obviously influencing our lives, right there in our very own living room.

Is television evil? Certainly no more evil than your microwave oven is evil. Justin Wise explains the sense in which the medium is the message:

> Think of it this way: Writing a letter by hand creates a different end product than when you write the same note in an email. There is something about a handwritten note that conveys intentionality, love, kindness, and warmth that gets lost on a computer screen. A note is tangible, tactile, and carries with it some essence of the sender. . . . Entire professions have evolved around analyzing handwriting, and for good reason. It reveals a great deal about a person.[1]

Television isn't evil, but it is powerful. Even the most trite television shows carry with them a subtle message: Life is about being entertained, and experiencing it vicariously through others is just as good as the real thing. Even amoral things can be used for good or evil. And they can be used too much or too little.

It is my contention that the convergence of social media and mobile devices has created a new wave of blind followers. Just as I had become a young disciple of Carl Winslow (*Family Matters*), Danny Tanner (*Full House*), and Phillip Banks (*The Fresh Prince of Bel-Air*) without knowing it, we are being influenced by a myriad of new and different voices through a number of different mediums every single day. We post, share, tweet, watch, listen, comment, snap, like, and message continually. We want to offer up our contribution to the ongoing conversation that is social media.

Is social media all bad? Certainly not. But perhaps we need to borrow a lesson from my grandfather and amble into the living room of our hearts with a different set of more discerning eyes. We should think carefully about the nature of this incredibly popular technology, the changes that are taking place in society, and our current habits of engagement.

There really aren't simple answers for how to navigate the digital wave that's swept us up and benefits us in some ways. What's clear is that we need to think carefully and critically about our use of social media. This book won't answer every issue, question, or problem about social media. Instead, I am hoping to bring to light some pertinent issues, uncover some basic problems, and ask some important questions based on my observations and research. I will offer some suggestions throughout, intentionally grounded in the good news of the gospel.

The first part of the book focuses on thinking critically about the medium of social media along with other advances in technology. I do my best to objectively describe where we are as a society with social media. To that end, it was imperative for me to pull away from using it every day, so I deactivated my social media accounts for one year. My goal was to be able to see the issue with fresh eyes. I wanted to be able to see clearly, as that local pastor had many years ago.

In some ways, my fears were confirmed during this time. In other ways, my hope for my church and for my children has brightened. In part one, you will probably find some things that concern you as well as some things that should encourage you. My prayer is that you will feel more equipped to approach the world around you with eyes wide open. Everyone benefits when we become more aware of the ramifications of our actions, because it allows us to change course.

There are some statistics in this book, but I am no researcher or statistician. There are some psychological evaluations that are presumed, but I am no psychologist. This book was born out of a single desire: I want to see the people in my church engaging with social media in a way that is consistent with a gospel worldview, and so I try to be faithful to that purpose throughout the book.

The second part of this book takes what I have observed about social media along with some statistics, and then lays a gospel lens over the top of it. Pastorally speaking, knowledge is good, but wisdom is best. To know information is always helpful, but to be empowered by the Holy Spirit to walk according to that knowledge is what we're after.

To achieve that objective, I will attempt to categorize some of the pitfalls of social media and explain how with gospel intentionality they can be overcome while preserving the positive aspects. My goal is not to be a social media critic, but to chart the course for utilizing social media as a tool for good.

With that goal in mind, I will apply Scriptural principles to the questions at hand: How should we interact online? What are the Lord's desires for us as we utilize this tool? How can we avoid some of the drawbacks we have all experienced?

Although the Bible was written in a world without social media and the Internet, it speaks through the centuries directly to the most pressing issues of our day.

Christians cannot simply be passive participants in culture. We should lean into our commission from Christ and thoughtfully engage with this new form of communication and community. Author and Christian missiologist Ed Stetzer reminds us, "It is both necessary and dangerous to engage culture."[2] We cannot ignore the dangers, but we should not neglect the opportunity either.

My hope and prayer is that readers will find real help in these pages for navigating the digital sea of social media through the truth of the gospel.

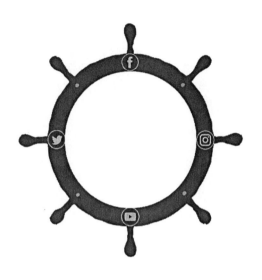

PART ONE
GETTING OUR BEARINGS

DIGITAL SEA:
THE UNSPOKEN AGREEMENT

Don't ever take a fence down until you know why it was put up.

—G.K. Chesterton

I grew up in a world without social media. I remember the robotic sounds of America Online (AOL) as my sister logged on when I was a child. Picking up the phone would "kick you off" the Internet, and nothing made my brother and me happier than doing just that as she spent time chatting away on AOL Instant Messenger (AIM).

It wasn't until my college years that I was introduced to the phenomenon called Facebook. At the time, Facebook was only open to college students, and it required having an email address attached to a university URL. It seemed fun and pretty exclusive, which added to its allure.

In high school, I had a few friends who tried to get me to join a social media site called MySpace. I wasn't the least bit interested. Something about ranking my top eight friends and posting pictures of myself didn't attract me. But Facebook was different. It seemed functional and possibly able to help me connect with new friends at college, so I went for it. Setting up my profile was pretty simple. Soon I was searching for a list of favorite books and quotes that would make me seem smarter and cooler than I actually was. Before long, I was adding new friends and investigating other people's pages. Two hours passed quickly, and going to Government 1301 was out of the question. Instead, I worked on adding photos to my page. It was just so easy to lose track of time.

Digital Maximalists

Many of you could tell a similar story about your entrance to social media. Slowly and steadily social media has become a huge part of our everyday lives. Facebook is now a multibillion-dollar business with over a billion users worldwide. It is no longer an exclusive "college only" site. New sites have been created like Instagram, Snapchat, Twitter, YouTube, Pinterest, Tumblr, Periscope, and more. Each of these sites has a unique place in the social media landscape, changing how we receive information and communicate with others. Along with this technological revolution, we have developed some deeply rooted ideas about life without recognizing it.

William Powers calls us "digital maximalists." He asserts:

Our philosophy has two corollaries.

First corollary: The more you connect, the better off you are.

Second corollary: The more you disconnect the worse off you are.[1]

With all the new online communal opportunities, we have embraced the idea that connectedness is to be pursued at all cost and that disconnectedness is to be avoided at all cost. Powers explains:

> We never sat down and consciously decided that this was the code we would live by. There was no discussion, no referendum or show of hands. It just sort of happened, as if by tacit agreement or silent oath. From now on, I will strive to be as connected as possible at all times. Like everyone else, I signed right on. I've spent most of the last decade within arm's length of a computer or my phone, usually both. When I was away from technology or when I just couldn't get a signal, I perceived it as a problem. If a hotel didn't have broadband in the room, I got irritated and complained. When I found myself in a region without cell phone coverage, I felt my provider had let me down. Staying with cousins for the holidays in a house without a wireless router, and thus no Internet connection for my laptop, I would go into the backyard or sit in the car on the street and try to pick up a neighbor's signal. Not once or twice a day, but many times. How else was I supposed to know what was going on in my life?[2]

I find Powers's analysis of his experience to be not only insightful, but also a necessary wake-up call.

As I mentioned, I took a sabbatical from social media in order to pull back a bit while working on this project. I don't consider myself to be a hyper-disciplined person, but I have always felt that if I made up my mind about something, it was as good as done. My sabbatical did not disprove this altogether, but it definitely raised some questions in my mind and heart about the significant ties that social media has to my desires and daily routine.

Within the first day of my social media sabbatical, I realized that my routines were greatly affected. I usually woke up to the sound of my alarm (on my phone), turned it off, and then rolled out of bed. Immediately I checked emails, responded to nighttime texts, and tapped my Twitter app to check the news cycle. One of my most entrenched habits immediately became glaringly obvious to me: Twitter had become as common to my morning routine as brushing my teeth.

By lunch, I recognized how often I instinctively clicked my Facebook tab on my home screen on breaks (and not on breaks) at my desk. It was a bit embarrassing to find myself staring at a log-in screen and remembering that my profile was deactivated. Soon, the disconnected feeling that Powers described above was upon me. Fear of missing out (FOMO) was in full effect, and its urgency surprised me. By the end of the first week, I had clicked on a social media application on my mobile device or laptop well over ten times a day by accident. I was beginning to realize that my experiment would be much harder than I had originally thought.

> I felt the fear of being forgotten.

I also began to experience a kind of inward tug pulling me back to the social media community. My FOMO was definitely a part of this tug, and another part of me missed being able to let others in on my life. I not only felt that I was going to miss out on everyone else's major life happenings, but that they might actually miss out on mine. I wasn't going to be able to update anyone on what was going in my world. I felt the fear of being forgotten.

Oddly enough, though, the tug I experienced most wasn't about any of that. It was something else. I genuinely missed the idea of having some general knowledge about everyone else. Social media had given me a certain sense of knowing what was going on in the lives of others. I knew who was married, who was dating, who was having babies, who was working out and at what gym. I knew people's political positions, friends' eating habits, church members' opinions, and old classmates' places of employment.

It's not that I was necessarily stalking all of these people (although that's a slippery slope I may have been down a time or two). This information was literally available to me at the tip of my fingers as I scrolled through my daily feed. Missing this sense of being "in the know" was the strongest tug pulling me back. I realized I really liked that feeling; conversely, being "out of the know" felt the way Powers had described—unsettling and incomplete.

This hunger for omniscience was a real and powerful drive in my life. I could never have vocalized it at the time, but in retrospect, knowing as much as I could about as many people as I could gave me a false sense of control and the illusion that I had a grasp on the world around me. The absence of that knowledge not only left me feeling less informed, but also less secure.

The book *The Circle* by Dave Eggers is about a dystopian future in which a social media tech company begins to change the way society as a whole operates. The novel's protagonist, Mae, is a regular girl who gets the opportunity to work for the famed company "Circle." Upon joining the tech company, she is pushed by superiors and coworkers to be more and more connected. An expectation to work in the Circle is that you are to be as connected as possible and to always be in the know. In a moment of reflection, Mae experiences the gnawing anxiety that describes how I have felt at times:

> It occurred to [Mae], in a moment of sudden clarity, that what had always caused her anxiety, or stress, or worry, was not any one force, nothing independent and external—it wasn't danger to herself or the constant calamity of other people and their problems. It was internal: it was subjective: it was not knowing.[3]

The not knowing is what was really getting to me, and I didn't expect that.

Soon, I had developed new go-to sites for news, and my goal-oriented mind had kicked into gear, seeking new things to focus on during my social media hiatus. I shirked the tug to be in the know by finding new things to know, and I was beginning to understand the cost of seeking omniscience.

I don't know exactly how or when my addiction to social media began. Perhaps it was that fateful day as a freshman in college when I proudly typed in my new university email to Facebook. Or maybe the roots of it began earlier with too much TV or with teasing my sister about her AIM accounts. In any case, at some point I signed on to the unspoken contract: Connectedness is good; disconnectedness is bad. And I have lived that way ever since.

The Digital Sea

I remember my first time going to a water park. My family and I went to Splashtown in Houston, Texas, and I couldn't have been more excited. Splashtown is a local, glorious mecca of summer enjoyment for children. Multiple acres of water slides, giant pools, fountains, and rivers were located all over the park. Excitement and laughter mixed with an occasional scream could be heard from the parking lot. By all accounts, this was the place to be.

The week leading up to our visit, my parents had prepared me for the worst. The forecast was gloomy, and the possibility of a rainout seemed likely. It's one of my first memories of praying. I asked God every day that week to hold back the rain and let the freedom of summertime ring.

When the big day arrived, to my great delight, sunshine was all I saw. My mind was racing with all of the possibilities for the day. There were so many rides and so little time. I was small, but just tall enough to inch over the surfboard height requirements. My brother and I went from ride to ride as he pressured me to go down slides that I was way too afraid to go down alone.

After a good few hours of running and swimming, we made our way to the wave pool. The wave pool is an innocent-looking ride as it connects to the calm Lazy River and looks relatively docile as you first approach it. People were lying back in their floats, playing with toddlers in the pool, and giving unsuspecting viewers the impression that all was calm and peaceful in the world.

I waded into the pool, ducked my head under the 3–4 feet of water, and blew air out of my nose as I felt the cold moisture on my sunburned face. It was great.

As my head was underwater I heard a siren sound.

As I emerged from the water, I was welcomed to an entirely different scene. The parents and toddlers were gone. I was surrounded by older kids screaming and laughing. The 3–4 feet of water was now 5–6 feet deep, and I could no longer touch the bottom. Then came the first wave.

For the next 10 minutes, I was gasping for breath and purposely going underwater so I could push off the bottom to gasp for another breath. I couldn't see my brother, and I wasn't sure I was going to make it. What started as a nice, underwater swim had turned into an aquatic nightmare.

We are being drowned by the waves of technological advancement in a digital sea. Social media is often as inviting as the wave pool before the siren. Understandably, we jumped right in to join the fun, but are now realizing we may have a lot to learn about navigating this new water we have found ourselves in. The waves are crashing and no one sounded the alarm.

If we're going to stay afloat, we're going to have to carefully examine the unwritten rules that are dictating our online lives.

Is it true that connectedness is good and disconnectedness is bad? If not, is the reverse true?

I had a hunch about some things that I still needed to confirm. Social media is a relatively new medium, but I figured there had to be some people out there who had done some research on the subject and had arrived at some helpful conclusions. This led me to explore some interesting information about new technology and the nature of people.

Reflection Questions

Is the unspoken agreement of connectivity a driving force in your life? How does this play out?

How has the desire to be "in the know" affected your use of social media?

Do you feel you have a decent grip on your social media use? Do you have any concerns?

PERSPECTIVE:
FACTS AND OBSERVATIONS

"I tried to put things in perspective but sometimes you're just too close to it."

—Cormac McCarthy

I was standing on top of a volcano. Even the thought of it was surreal. I had climbed over 12,000 feet into the Guatemalan sky, struggling the whole way. The last 2,000 feet or so were entirely through ash. Every step I took in that last leg of the journey punched my foot shin-deep in soot, causing me to inch up the mountain.

This was our first mission trip together, and my wife and I had not packed everything we needed for the hike. The guides were bounding up ahead of us as we panted and heaved to the halfway point. Why had I declined the donkey that was offered to me at the trailhead for the first half of our trek? In hindsight, it was only because of pride. Now I was paying the price.

As I stood atop the volcano and looked out over the landscape, the searing in my legs began to fade and my heavy breathing subsided. There was a wonderful calm up there. It was as if someone had opened a window and let all the fresh air rush into my lungs.

The feeling of accomplishment you get after making it through a daunting test of perseverance felt great, but the view was even greater. I could see for what seemed like miles and miles. The vastness of the countryside was before me, and from my vantage point high in the heavens, everything below was easy to place. Soft clouds dotted the sky with green pastures and winding roads beneath me. Even a foreigner could navigate his way around the area from this vantage point. I could see everything around me, and all the potential obstacles to avoid on the trip down the volcano were in clear view. It was incredible.

Perspective is necessary to chart a wise course for our online journey. It is not enough for us to assume we know where the pitfalls are located; we must reach a vantage point that will allow us to survey the entire landscape. We must humble ourselves and acknowledge that we are all foreigners here, and charting the course ahead should not be left to trial and error. There is too much at stake to waste our time wandering aimlessly without a map of the territory.

Returning to our nautical theme, remember the movie *Titanic*? One of the most popular movies of our time is also one of the greatest tragedies of a former time. The story goes that the unsinkable ship met its demise because of an immovably large iceberg in the Atlantic. Thousands lost their lives, and Rose wouldn't let Jack join her on the headboard even though it was clearly large enough for the two of them.

But, remember, that wasn't the whole story. The true story behind the story was the captain of the ship being urged by others to steam ahead. "The ship is unsinkable. Why concern ourselves with caution? Just plow through if you must!" he reasoned.

Many of us bring this same mentality to some areas of our lives. We plow ahead, throwing caution to the wind, thinking our plans are quite unsinkable.

In my time away from social media I was able to gain a fresh perspective. Plowing full steam ahead without caring to slow down isn't the answer. So, I pulled away and climbed up the ashy volcano to get a better look at the landscape below. There is something empowering about making the steep climb to get a better vantage point.

Below are my observations from that higher vantage point along with supporting facts obtained from helpful guides who have done their own exploratory work.

Observations: Social media encourages busyness in my soul. I waste time on social media.

Fact: We spend a lot of time online and on social media.

As I mentioned, I noticed an anxiety in me on the first day of not being connected. It's like that feeling you get when you are going on a vacation, get to the airport, and sense you are missing something. It keeps nagging at you. I was missing my connectedness, and I couldn't shake the feeling that something was off—because it was . . . I was off.

> The more and more disconnected
> I became, the more I realized the
> collective hurriedness of
> my peers.

After the first few weeks, though, which I considered my "detox phase," I began to notice other things. The more and more disconnected I became, the more I realized the collective hurriedness of my peers. Every time I went anywhere, phones were out, screens were lit, and people were immersed in the digital world. I noticed when people would come over for dinner or sit on my couch for coffee, they would sometimes begin scrolling through Facebook while I was talking to them.

I suppose that might have been because the conversation wasn't all that stimulating, which isn't out of the question. But the more I paid attention, the more I noticed similar incidents of inattention and non-presence taking place in a variety of ways and in a variety of places. For instance:

- A woman scrolling through Facebook as she runs on the treadmill.
- A man scrolling Instagram in the movie theater (as the movie played).
- A teenage girl Snapchatting during class to a friend sitting right next to her.
- A grieving family member updating profile pictures during her uncle's funeral.

Of course, there could be mitigating explanations in some of these examples. The treadmill is pretty monotonous, so perhaps I can give her a pass. And maybe the man hated the "chick flick" his wife made him go to and was just trying to pass the time. Nonetheless, I noticed a weird busyness that seemed to be the direct result of social media obsession. From the moment we wake up to the moment we go to bed, we are always expected to be connected. This reality was driven home to me during the second month of my social media hiatus.

I had not appropriately warned others of my time away, and therefore there were multiple people who were offended at my ignoring them online. Of course, I wasn't intending this effect, but it revealed part of the reason we are all so busy—thousands of online friends expect us to like, comment, post, tweet, retweet, heart, favorite, and respond to them immediately or sooner! This unspoken agreement of connectivity brings with it a hefty sense of responsibility.

The numbers tell the story. According to one study, the average person spends about 26 hours per week online.[1] To me this number seemed low, and there are other studies suggesting much higher numbers, but I wanted to go with a conservative estimate. The graph below shows how we divvy up our time in a typical week between being online and doing other things. The numbers might be a little surprising to some, but it doesn't seem too unreasonable given the way we've embraced the connected life. (Incidentally, the uncritical acceptance of connectivity can lead to rationalizing our online lives when we feel a pang of guilt about it.)

Time spent online   **Time spent other**

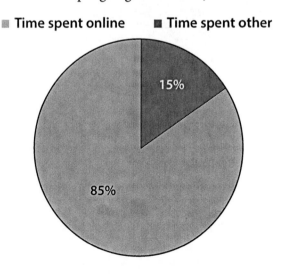

15%

85%

The next graph brings some additional clarity. Assuming an average 40-hour workweek and an average of 8 hours of sleep per night, our remaining uncommitted time has shrunk considerably. What initially seems like a healthy surplus of free time now looks a lot less open. Only 18 percent of our weekly hours remain free. Unless we rethink the level of connectivity in our lives, our sense of margin will quickly disappear.

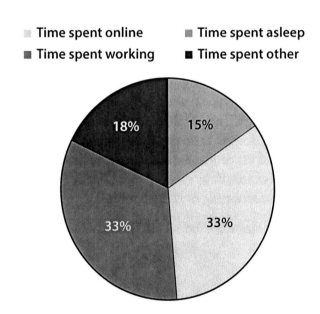

Of course, not all of us get a full 8 full hours of sleep a night. And others of us might be able to get some online connectivity time out of the way at work (whether authorized or not), but these shortcuts probably aren't possible or wise in the long term.

My estimation of our true available time would take into

account a number of other responsibilities most of us have to varying degrees. For instance, the number of hours spent running children to and from school, commuting to and from work, driving to practices, games, and other extracurricular activities, various appointments, night school for a graduate degree, car and home maintenance, and staying in touch with others in non-social media ways, just to name a few. Add to all of that the constant buzzing in your pocket, keeping you up to date with all the messages you must respond to and the people who require a comment or a like and you can begin to see the problem. At times, your sleep might be interrupted by the social media crew nudging you to stay up after hours. A study by researchers at the University of Pittsburgh School of Medicine suggests that "heavy social media use could wreak havoc with your sleep patterns."[2] That's not the least bit surprising. The call of connectivity is loud, and creates a constant sense that we're never truly offline and we can never truly rest.

In the busyness and chaos, we begin to ask ourselves the question: Where will I find the time to do all this stuff? And we usually don't have an answer.

While details may vary, most of us have felt the busyness of life and the burden of connectivity, even though we enjoy it on some level, too. With the realization that we are active online and that it does take up a lot of our time, we mustn't foolishly tell the captain to speed up the ship when we have been warned of icebergs! The danger is here, and we must learn to navigate it because there aren't enough lifeboats of time and margin for us to live sane and purposeful lives apart from exercising significant caution and wisdom.

Observation: People say things on social media that they would never say in person.

Fact: Many people act differently online than they do in real life.

Observation: Social media is a breeding ground for narcissism.

Fact: Narcissism and the use of social media are inextricably linked.

We have all experienced that moment. We opened our app or web browser in the morning to discover a friend or acquaintance has gone overboard with an online rant about something or someone. We read the cringe worthy statements made in haste. We sift through the comments, finding approval from some while others try to ease the unhinged poster in a more helpful and healthy direction. We wonder if we should enter into the controversy or leave it alone. And we wonder how this person can be so inconsiderate and outspoken online, but thoughtful and reserved in person?

> "Over one-third of [our] waking hours are spent on our mobile devices."

Keith Wilcox from Columbia University asserts that social media users tend to present a positive self-view to others: "Think of it as a licensing effect: You feel good about yourself so you feel a sense of entitlement."[3]

The rise of social media is correlated to a rise in narcissism. The "selfie culture" did not come into existence out of nothing. We create online profiles that project the best image of ourselves, including using the best picture we can find. We then proceed to post status updates, engage in comment sections, and dialogue with others based on the projection or desired persona we've attempted to create.

We can be like the man in *The Wizard of Oz*—not very impressive in person, but living behind a huge façade, projecting the image of a strong, powerful wizard to the world. Despite all our talk of authenticity, we are very frequently tempted to live behind the curtain, pulling the strings and putting on the show.

When others like our status updates, it affirms the value of the projection we have created. People approve of us, and they have shown it by their likes. As we carve out a place in our online community, our self-esteem rises in concert with the likability of the projection of ourselves we've created. Soon, we are bolder and more outspoken within our online community than anywhere else because we feel confident that our voice will be heard and appreciated there.

Going back to Wilcox's thesis that connectedness is *assumed* to always be good, we don't need a large leap of imagination to see how increasing narcissism (self-focus) can lead to entitlement (an expected response), which, at its worst, creates the "troll culture."

"Trolls" are online antagonizers. They wiggle their way into every conversation and comment section on social media to create tension and start arguments. Trolls like to create controversy and stir the pot. In *Time* magazine, Joel Stein discusses these trolls:

Internet trolls have a manifesto of sorts, which states they are doing it for the "lulz," or laughs. What trolls do for the lulz ranges from clever pranks to harassment to violent threats. There's also doxxing—publishing personal data, such as Social Security numbers and bank accounts—and swatting, calling in an emergency to a victim's house so the SWAT team busts in. When victims do not experience lulz, trolls tell them they have no sense of humor. Trolls are turning social media and comment boards into a giant locker room in a teen movie, with towel-snapping racial epithets and misogyny.[4]

Trolls represent narcissistic social media engagement at its worst. So self-absorbed, so entitled, and so out of touch with reality that they have created their own set of online etiquette to follow—namely, none at all.

But, remember, trolls aren't created out of nothing. They are molded out of our consistent love of self. A recent example is Kim Kardashian's book *Selfish,* which is a photo collage of her personal favorite selfies. The book is all about *her.*

Clearly, the thirst for approval is very real, and social media allows us to seek out the approval we crave in one easy click. And if we aren't successful at first, that's not a problem. We just need to tweak the projection a bit until we find something that works. Soon, we discover what our audience likes, and we are on the fast track to receiving the applause we desperately desire. And it's such an easy fix to our self-esteem. We aren't actually required to change our character, just the online character we're playing. It's much easier to sustain a way of life online because of how impersonal it is. And we don't need to have everyone online approve of us to get what we need; we just need to find an online niche where others will cheer us on.

I must admit, I noticed the narcissism in others first, and then in myself, which is a textbook narcissist move. No one is immune from the temptation of inordinate or illegitimate self-love.

Stepping back from the online community didn't just mean getting away from the noise; it also meant giving up the applause. Soon, I was no longer inundated with congratulations on my birthday, or likes on my pictures and status updates. As a pastor, it wasn't as easy for me to receive an "attaboy" for good sermons or to see others quote my words from last week's message on their page. No one was retweeting my pithy 140-character thought bubbles. It didn't crush me, but it did matter to me more than I thought it would.

It is a humbling thing to have your heart unveiled and find inappropriate self-love. But sometimes a little humbling is what we need most.

Observations: Our connectivity has crowded our hearts and numbed us. We struggle with silence.

Case Study: Andrew Sullivan.

Andrew Sullivan is a successful writer and blogger who considers himself to be an early adopter to the Internet. Being a successful online entrepreneur required a lot of work from Sullivan, and all of that work was *connected* work. That didn't repel Sullivan, however. Instead, he threw himself into it, heart and soul. He joked with friends that "if the Internet can kill you, I will be the first to find out."[5]

In a fascinating self-discovery piece, Sullivan shared the process he went through of realizing the seriousness of his distraction and information overload addiction. Sullivan discovered, as I had, that his connectivity had become a big problem in his life. In his research, he came across a particularly jarring stat: "Over one-third of [our] waking hours are spent on our mobile devices."[6]

He knew something had to change, so he booked himself at a retreat center to detox from constant connection (a much more intense version of my experiment). He describes how he felt after a couple days there:

> And then, unexpectedly, on the third day, as I was walking through the forest, I became overwhelmed. I'm still not sure what triggered it, but my best guess is that the shady, quiet woodlands, with brooks trickling their way down hillsides and birds flitting through the moist air, summoned memories of my childhood. I was a lonely boy who spent many hours outside in the copses and woodlands of my native Sussex, in England. I had explored this landscape with friends, but also alone— playing imaginary scenarios in my head, creating little nooks where I could hang and sometimes read, learning every little pathway through the woods and marking each flower or weed or fungus that I stumbled on. But I was also escaping a home where my mother had collapsed with bipolar disorder after the birth of my younger brother and had never really recovered. She was in and out of hospitals for much of my youth and adolescence, and her condition made it hard for her to hide her pain and suffering from her sensitive oldest son.
>
> I absorbed a lot of her agony, I came to realize later, hearing her screams of frustration and misery in

constant, terrifying fights with my father, and never knowing how to stop it or to help. I remember watching her dissolve in tears in the car picking me up from elementary school at the thought of returning to a home she clearly dreaded, or holding her as she poured her heart out to me, through sobs and whispers, about her dead-end life in a small town where she was utterly dependent on a spouse. She was taken away from me several times in my childhood, starting when I was 4, and even now I can recall the corridors and rooms of the institutions she was treated in when we went to visit.

It was as if, having slowly and progressively removed every distraction from my life, I was suddenly faced with what I had been distracting myself from. Resting for a moment against the trunk of a tree, I stopped, and suddenly found myself bent over, convulsed with the newly present pain, sobbing.[7]

After three days of forced disconnectedness, Andrew was brought face-to-face with an important truth. We are more than an online profile of names, favorite books, hobbies, and pithy quotes. We are made in the image of God, and there is depth to the human soul.

Sullivan was ultra-connected to the online world, boasting thousands of friends and followers, but in the meantime he had lost connection with his own soul. In all that connectivity there was a short-circuit that only silence and solitude could repair. In the silence, he was met with something we all must face or medicate—our deep brokenness.

As we are let into Sullivan's encounter with his brokenness, it can feel a little too close for comfort. When real pain is so up close and personal, our first reaction might be to cover our eyes and ears and head for the exits. We are culturally uncomfortable with grief and suffering, and therefore when ugly pain rears its head, we want to ignore it or somehow escape it.

Social media allows for relationships on our terms. Without the physical component of looking another person in the eye, we can back away from the suffering we see online without anyone noticing our absence. This encourages us to do the same with our own brokenness. Rather than address it and feel the pain it can bring, we ignore it. We run away from it and hide ourselves in the virtual world.

This virtual world can numb us, but it can never heal us. It is like an IV drip, not a physician. It took Andrew Sullivan just three days to realize how easy it is to crowd our hearts with noise. I know he's not the only one who needs to make that discovery.

Observations: Online community is a façade and undermines real community.

Fact: The research is inconclusive.

The decline of community in our society began before the onset of social media, so it is difficult to correlate the two with any scientific exactness. Nevertheless, Robert Putnam wrote a prophetic work in 2000 called *Bowling Alone,* which catalogued the declining value of community in America. Putnam said something in that book that seems to agree with my observation:

"Social capital may turn out to be a prerequisite for, rather than a consequence of, effective computer-mediated communication."[8]

In other words, he believed that relationships in real life (non-computer-mediated) had to be the basis for effective online community. He suggested that if we tried to center our communal and relational lives online, we would be deeply disappointed. We would find ourselves wanting something more.

There are some apparent positives to having mostly online friendships. You can get to know others across time zones and even oceans. You don't have to be near someone to find a conversation partner, which can seem preferable sometimes. For those of us who struggle to find time—which is almost all of us—these relationships can feel less time-consuming. Also, online community has easier on and off ramps—logging out is easier than walking out.

Justin Wise, author of *The Social Church,* sums up how many feel about online community:

Dave is my former college roommate, and Twitter is one of his main relational lines I use to stay connected to him. He lives in Chicago. I live in Des Moines. While many of the relationships I formed at college have faded, Dave and I can still see what's going on with each other, 140 characters at a time. The next time we meet, we'll know, in part, some of the details of what's going on with each other. This is to be affirmed and celebrated. I'm able to go deeper faster with Dave the next time we connect.[9]

I generally agree with Wise's explanation. He goes on to assert that online community has its limitations and that "offline [community] always trumps online community," which I completely agree with.

My concern is that because we have heartily "affirmed and celebrated" online relationships both intentionally and unintentionally, we may be undermining the value of the very real community all around us. I often ignore my neighbor across the street while spending large amounts of time scanning online news feeds. I have frequently spoken inattentively to my coffee barista, face buried in my phone, choosing online information about online friends over a real-life interaction with a real-life person. We need to return to a hopeful and serious affirmation and celebration of life-on-life, face-to-face community.

> We need to return to a hopeful and serious affirmation and celebration of life-on-life, face-to-face. community.

The question is not whether it is more or less convenient. Online community is tons more convenient, as is online communication in general. But online community cannot take the place of real-life interactions. As Wise points out, "I can't break bread with you in a Facebook group. . . . I can't share in your sorrow or suffering in an online environment. I can get close, but there is an obvious threshold."[10]

Observations: Online community encourages unhealthy comparison.

Fact: The longer people search on Facebook, the worse they feel about their lives.

Serving as a church planter affords me the opportunity of watching young families grow. At one point, my wife and

I conducted almost twenty weddings in an 18-month span. This meant tons of pre-marital counseling, tons of prayer and preparations, tons of vows, rings, and pronouncements—and a year later, tons of babies.

Babies are a lot of fun and a lot of work. New moms are the most affected. Sleep schedules go awry and soon the cuddly human you prayed 9 months for has become a nuisance. Moms don't want to feel this way of course, but they do. And they have to decide whether they are going to admit it or mask it. Social media allows the platform for both.

I have coined this new pressure to stay on top of things Social Comparison Syndrome (SCS). New moms engaged online feel rising levels of expectations and responsibility. The online revolution has created a constant stream of new information about how they should be raising their children.

> Social Comparison Syndrome (SCS)
> is the unhealthy habit of online
> comparison that creates bitterness,
> disdain, or pride.

Passive-aggressive, competitive exchanges are not uncommon among new moms these days. They have to keep up with latest scientific discoveries, new diet methods, most recent blog posts, and best child-rearing practices. All of this while deciding between:

- cloth diapers or Huggies
- natural births or medicinal
- organic vs. non-organic food

- breastfeeding vs. the bottle
- home school vs. public vs. private

And then social media enters the picture and SCS is created. As moms try to figure out how to do it all, they take to the social media stratosphere to begin posting opinions and updating the world on their findings. As the kids grow older, social media can be a reminder to many moms of what they aren't doing right. They see others' lives, parenting styles, play dates, and field trips posted online with the perfect picture filter. Other people's children always seem well-behaved, happy, and healthy. They can't help but feel deficient as they pick up their messy, disobedient, and sometimes sick children from daycare.

> So we are all trying to present the best versions of ourselves possible, but are simultaneously all discouraged. Everyone else seems to have it together while our lives seem so mundane, muddled and outright messy.

Or if they are actually doing pretty well, they may struggle not to boast about it before the world or feel superior around other mothers who "just can't seem to figure it out." Either way, SCS has done damage to people and relationships.

SCS is the unhealthy habit of online comparison that creates bitterness, disdain, or pride. It's certainly not unique to moms. My pastoral experience with moms highlighted it for me, but the condition affects all genders, roles, and age groups. A study in Utah in 2001 showed:

Those who have used Facebook longer agreed more that others were happier, and agreed less that life is fair, and those spending more time on Facebook each week agreed more that others were happier and had better lives.[11]

In other words, SCS is an issue across the board. We look online, see the highlight reels of others, and come to the conclusion that life is unfair and others are happier than us. The same study asserted what we already mentioned above: "People tend to present themselves in a favorable way on their Facebook profile."[12]

We are all trying to present the best versions of ourselves possible, but are simultaneously all discouraged. Everyone else seems to have it together while our lives seem so mundane, muddled, and messy. There was one indicator of a variable in the experiment. They found that "those that included more people whom they did not personally know as their Facebook 'friends' agreed more that others had better lives."[13]

That means that people who had real-life community and real-life relationships that were *supplemented* by their online life were less affected by SCS than those who had more friends that they didn't actually spend time with day-to-day in person. Putnam's theory seems to have been confirmed by these findings. Real, tangible, life-on-life community as the basis for online community helps safeguard us from unhealthy comparison.

Observations: Social Media scratches the itch for approval that we all have deep down.

Fact: Human beings are hard-wired for self-disclosure and social approval, and social media is the perfect platform for both.

When I was a young child, I was known in my household for having a great memory. As I mentioned earlier, my television and movie addiction started young, and therefore so did my memorization of movie lines. I watched *Homeward Bound* every day after school for my entire year of Kindergarten. Shadow, Sassy, and Chance had no lines that I did not know by heart.

One of our family favorites was *Independence Day* with Will Smith. No one can deny Will Smith's hold on the '90s generation, and I was no exception. My parents used to get a laugh out of watching the film and having me mimic the words as they were being spoken. Sometimes they would turn the television off and ask me to continue on my own, reciting the lines to them in front of the screen. After a while they would turn the TV back on to see if I was still on track with the movie. When my words and pauses were spot-on matches to the film, they would burst out clapping and cheering.

I ate it up.

Even as a child, I loved to be celebrated. I worked hard to get better at activities, sports, and academics in order to be praised. I had a great relationship with my coaches because I worked hard for a simple pat on the back.

This is clearly not unique to me, and it wasn't all bad to desire some affirmation and praise. We should all celebrate our children as I was celebrated as a child because that is the way that God celebrates over us. But there is a darker side to this itch in our soul to be praised, and it has some even darker origins.

Social media is the perfect platform to capitalize on this universal hunger in the human soul to receive attention and praise. In a *New York Times* article, Bruce Feiler says this:

> A growing body of research indicates how deeply our brains are wired to seek social approval. A study out of Harvard in 2012 showed that humans devote up to 40 percent of our time to self-disclosure, and doing so is as pleasurable as having food or sex. Diana Tamir and Jason Mitchell gave people small cash rewards for answering factual questions and lower rewards for offering their own views about a subject. Despite the financial incentive, people preferred to talk about themselves and willingly gave up money to do so.[14]

Since we all love to be praised and long for it often, it is very easy to see why a digital online community that is built around mutual affirmation would attract us. When we "like" something on social media, we are acknowledging it or even praising it. When we share something, we are affirming that we have found it worthy to let our circle of influence see it, too. When we retweet something, it is just like quoting someone. When we see someone "heart" something on Instagram, it is as though they have personally complemented something about us.

All of these actions have an element of praise to them.

On the other hand, *not* receiving these online praises can be devastating. Feiler adds,

> In a study he did with his wife, Naomi Eisenberger, Mr. Lieberman monitored subjects' brains while having them play a video game in which they tossed a ball with

two others. But the two others were avatars, and they quickly stopped sharing the ball with the subject. The pain the subjects felt at being cut out was devastating, on par with breaking a leg.[15]

The stakes are raised for praise in the social media realm. Being affirmed on a public forum can give you as much joy as eating a fantastic meal or even having intimate relations with your spouse. Yet, being ignored and neglected in the online coliseum can cause you to experience bone-breaking pain.

The Bible has a term for our hearts' deepest desire: *glory.* Our hearts long for glory, and moments of human praise can give us temporary satisfaction but will ultimately cause us to long for more. This explains why athletes struggle to retire despite their many career achievements. And it explains the tenacity with which Olympians push through the pain of grueling workouts from such a young age. All of this is done in the hope of hearing the applause and experiencing the glory we long for.

> Social media is the perfect platform to capitalize on this universal hunger in the human soul to receive attention and praise.

It was true for me as a small child standing in front of our enormous cube television, and it is true of you as you read this sentence today. We are hungry for glory, and social media is like a fast-food option set out before us.

Perspective

Looking out over the mountainous, green terrain of Antigua was an incredible experience. The perspective from up there was truly breathtaking. There's a downside to only having a bird's-eye view, though. As I looked down into the valleys below, the houses and huts all kind of looked alike. Gas stations and grocery stores were just two similar tiny dots. It is harder to distinguish things from so far away.

It reminded me of something my grandfather told me during my first time deer hunting.

In Texas, deer hunting is a favorite pastime, and I started at 9 years old. We were seated in our deer stand at 4:30 a.m. The cold, still air froze my tiny ears even though they were underneath my toboggan. Fog hung over the icy pond as we both stared silently into the morning darkness, listening closely for any movement. As the sun rose, I saw something move far off in the distance. I jerked, and pulled the stock to my shoulder to take aim. My grandfather gripped my wrist tightly. He slowly and deliberately aimed his gun, peered through the scope and then smirked at me.

It was a cow.

After the disappointment and shame had settled on my face, he looked at me wisely and said, "Don't worry, son. Everything looks like a deer from a few hundred yards away."

A bird's-eye view isn't enough to fully understand social media. We need some real-life stories from the ground to get the full picture.

THE GOOD, THE BAD, THE UGLY

"Storytelling reveals meaning without committing the error of defining it."

—Hannah Arendt

The Good

In 2010, a young man named Jay Jaboneta[1] was surfing Facebook, as he was apt to do. As a young Filipino, he had been conversing with a friend about the country's presidential elections when he heard some news that shocked him.

Five-hundred miles south of Manilla, Philippines, there is a small town called Layag-Layag. This small agricultural community is full of seaweed farmers. The children of this town spend their mornings as you might expect—getting dressed, packing their book bags, and rushing out the door for school. Nothing unusual about that. However, there is some extra packing the Layag-Layag children must do every morning; they have to pack plastic bags for their school clothes.

Each morning they pack up and head out for a 2-kilometer swim to school. They wear one set of clothes that they know will get wet and dirty on the trek, and switch over to their school uniforms once they reach dry enough land. Then they repeat the process on the way home.

Jay was moved by these children's plight. He decided to do what many of us do when we are rattled by injustice. He shared it online. His status read,

Wow . . . kids swim 2km to school!!!

Not a very heartfelt or moving status, but it garnered a big response anyway.

> Jay had met a real need for real people, and he had done so through the power of social media.

He began to get replies from others who wanted to help. After some dialogue online, Jay set up a way to give. A week later, he had $1,600 to help build a boat for these children. A pretty impressive response. Jay had met a real need for real people, and he had done so through the power of social media. Even more importantly, he had made it easier for children to get the education they need.

In this way, the Yellow Boat Foundation of Hope was born.

But as is often the case, the issue was more complicated than he originally thought. It didn't take long for Jay to realize that a boat wasn't enough. Although having water transportation in the morning was incredibly helpful, when the tide went out in the afternoon, the children were still having to walk through 2 kilometers' worth of muddy waterbeds on the way home. By getting closer to the situation, Jay realized that the deeper issue was poverty and that the struggles this community faced couldn't be fully solved with simple yellow boats.

As Jay put it, "A boat was kind of useless. You can't just give whatever you think they need, you have to find out what their needs are."

So, that's what he set out to do. He began to engage the people at a personal level and find out their deeper needs. He learned that the solution tied into his initial hope for the yellow boats. This community needed a more holistic approach. He needed to help these high school students secure scholarships from the College of Marine Science and Technology so that they could come up with long-term solutions to their problems. For Jay, this was a key to helping improve the overall quality of life in the community.

From the one boat that he initially purchased by way of his unceremonious Facebook campaign, he has now used his presence on social media to raise money to send 1,200 boats and is an advocate for many students in the community. Yellow Boat now has fundraising chapters in the United States, Canada, Europe, and the Middle East. The volunteer-driven organization now serves thirty communities across the country.

Born and raised in Cotabato City, Jay was named by Yahoo! Southeast Asia in 2011 as one of the 7 Modern-Day Filipino Heroes for his involvement in the project Zamboanga Funds for Little Kids, which has been renamed as the Yellow Boat of Hope Foundation. His work with the project has been featured by Reader's Digest Asia / Indonesia / India, Associated Press (AP), CNN, BusinessWeek, Forbes, The Huffington Post, and other international and Philippine-based news organizations.[2]

Jay's work in the Philippines was made possible by a single status on social media. Jay recollects,

> A single Facebook status can make a difference. We sometimes take for granted what we share on social media—what we tweet or post on Facebook or Instagram—but our story really shows that you can start any good project from wherever you are. *You don't need to be very rich or connected. As long as you are passionate about it, it can happen* (emphasis mine).[3]

Jay's story serves as an example of social media's potential for good. Harnessing social media's power to quickly inform large numbers of people about a genuine need can be very effective in fighting injustice and bringing practical aid to those who need it. In this way, it serves as a great tool for furthering cooperation, mercy, and justice, sometimes achieving amazing results in a short period of time.

> Social media can be a tool that champions cooperation, mercy, and justice.

The Bad

We have all had that moment when we've said too much. Perhaps we took a joke too far, or maybe the meaning of our passionate explanation about something got muddled among our many words. Usually, we can backtrack or apologize, but not always.

In the case of Justine Sacco's slip of the tongue on Twitter,[4] no amount of hitting the brakes could stop the runaway train of her words from causing a lot of damage

It was a normal day for Justine as she prepared to travel overseas to visit family in South Africa for Christmas vacation. The senior director of corporate communications at IAC, she was funny and brash, and at times inappropriate. But she had no idea what her funny and brash side had in store for her in the upcoming flight hours.

She began by live-tweeting her conditions as she meandered through the international airport. For anyone who has traveled internationally, you can laugh knowingly at some of her observations as she made her way through lines and close proximity with others:

Weird German Dude: You're in First Class. It's 2014. Get some deodorant.—Inner monologue as I inhale BO. Thank God for pharmaceuticals.

> Justine's issue was not only that she made the comments, but where she made them from.

Her style was pretty edgy, but often the most successful American online media personalities are that way. I wouldn't consider most of her tweets overwhelmingly out of bounds. She landed in London and commented on the layover:

Chilly—cucumber sandwiches—bad teeth. Back in London!

As she made her way onto her last leg of the flight to vacation, she was about to make one of the most significant mistakes of her life. To be clear, her comment was definitely disparaging and ignorant. She was insensitive and inappropriate. However, I have personally been that way, too. Justine's issue was not only that she made the comments, but *where* she made them from:

Going to Africa. Hope I don't get AIDS. Just kidding. I'm white!

Now, cue the chaos.

With only 170 Twitter followers, Justine couldn't have imagined the backlash in store. Sure, she was a communications director, but she didn't think anyone significant would be paying attention. After all, who was going to take such an outrageous statement seriously, right? Wrong.

During the 11-hour flight time, Justine had become a top trending Twitter topic and had earned the ridicule of much of the Western world. She was deemed a bigot, racist, narcissist, and more. Once she landed, the text messages began to stream in as she tried to keep up with the narrative.

Soon she realized that what she thought was just a rather harmless tweet to her 170 followers had become headline news, confirming in the minds of many the arrogance of the US and her people. Justine was threatened, accused, and thrown into the all-too-familiar outrage blender of social media within hours of her terrible mistake. She went from a relatively unknown jokester to an infamous social pariah in less time than it takes to watch *The Lord of the Rings* trilogy.

The *New York Times* recorded some of the comments on her Twitter feed[5]:

In light of @Justine-Sacco disgusting racist tweet, I'm donating to @care today

How did @JustineSacco get a PR job?! Her level of racist ignorance belongs on Fox News. #AIDS can affect anyone!

I'm an IAC employee and I don't want @JustineSacco doing any communications on our behalf ever again. Ever.

This is an outrageous, offensive comment. Employee in question currently unreachable on an intl flight.

All I want for Christmas is to see @JustineSacco's face when her plane lands and she checks her inbox/voicemail

Oh man, @JustineSacco is going to have the most painful phone-turning-on moment ever when her plane lands

*We are about to watch this @JustineSacco ***** get fired. In REAL time. Before she even KNOWS she's getting fired.*

Most were not even this kind. Donald Trump even jumped in, calling for Justine to be fired. The important thing to note here is not that somehow Justine's tweet was justifiable. It certainly wasn't. However, the pile-on culture of social media played a big part in taking a wrong action, globalizing it, and creating a national pariah.

"I cried out my body weight in the first 24 hours," she told me. "It was incredibly traumatic. You don't sleep. You wake up in the middle of the night forgetting where you are. Unfortunately, I am not a character on 'South Park' or a comedian, so I had no business commenting on the epidemic in such a politically incorrect manner on a public platform."[6]

Justine was not your typical victim, but she definitely experienced suffering. She was not guaranteed safety upon landing in South Africa. Her hotel accommodations included hotel workers threatening to strike and protest her presence. Upon arrival at her family's home, she was chastised for her carelessness and how it had tarnished a good family name. She was bombarded with anger and hate. Carelessness had led to something much more deadly, and she never saw it coming.

It was a media outlet known for combustible stories, Gawker, that caused the tweet to gain traction. A writer received an anonymous tip about the tweet and hopped on the opportunity.

"The fact that she was a PR chief made it delicious," he wrote. "It's satisfying to be able to say, 'O.K., let's make a racist tweet by a senior IAC employee count this time.' And it did. I'd do it again."[7]

For Justine though, this was the beginning of a painstaking process. Her identity was forever tainted. She was now one of the most hated personalities, not only on social media, but in the media in general. She understood the uphill climb ahead. Her dating life, her occupational hopes and dreams (she was fired immediately), and even her family life were drastically different overnight.

> The margin for error can be razor-thin online, and the consequences can be life-altering.

Justine's story is clearly an exception, but many people experience social media much differently than Jay did. Remember Jay's status about children swimming 2 kilometers to school? It wasn't antagonistic, but it wasn't overly empathetic either. Yet it had a positive response that was greater than he could have expected. Narratives are written through the lens of the audience. The margin for error can be razor-thin online, and the consequences can be life-altering.

The Ugly

Amanda[8] was a normal seventh-grade girl who enjoyed talking with her friends online. She would join chatrooms and webcams and loved engaging the social scene. Like many teenagers, she became a little careless and used her webcam to meet "new people" online. The desire was harmless really, but the outcome was tragic.

She met a boy online. This young man said all of the right things and complimented her in all the right ways: "beautiful, stunning, perfect . . ." She was flattered. So when he asked her to show him her breasts on webcam the first time, she wasn't alarmed. He was so nice and complimentary to her. More importantly, he was interested. She didn't give in at first, but he was persistent, and after a while he wore her down. She knew it wasn't wise, but he seemed to really like her.

Soon afterwards, she was contacted on social media. He was threatening to show her photographs to everyone important in her life. The young man had all of her pertinent information, too—personal address, school address, classes, friends, family names, etc.—and taunted her with it. He said that if she refused to "put on a show" for him, she would have to face the consequence of public shame.

During Christmas break of 2010, her worst fears came true. The police informed Amanda that her photograph was circulating online. Amanda's recollection of the story speaks to her level of trauma. She began experiencing panic disorders, anxiety, and depression. Her family moved her to another school, where she admits to turning to drugs and alcohol to cope with her shame and embarrassment.

After a year, the man reappeared online, using topless images of Amanda as a profile picture and befriending her classmates on social media in order to destroy any relationships she may have made in her new school. The emotional toll this took on her was devastating. After being bullied in her new school again over the photos, she moved once more to try to escape the ridicule, attacks, and shame.

In the new place, Amanda was having some mild success in starting over. She began engaging with a young boy she deemed "an old friend" over the phone. Amanda was trying to find her footing as a normal young teen, pursuing romance with a boy her age. But, again, Amanda found herself in a difficult predicament. The young man was dating another girl, but he wanted Amanda to come over while the other girl was out of town. Amanda complied, and they engaged sexually with one another.

The week that followed proved to be catastrophic for young Amanda. Again, there's an element of teenage drama in her story that seems almost normal if it weren't so tragic. As the story unfolds, however, it becomes more and more clear that what's going on is more than teenage angst and some bad decisions.

The offended girl brought her group of friends to Amanda's school one afternoon to confront Amanda about her indiscretion.

"Can't you see that nobody likes you?" the girl said to Amanda in front of her peers at Amanda's third new school in a few short years. Amanda was pierced by her words.

"Just go ahead and punch her already!" a bystander yelled from the crowd.

The girls engaged in a physical altercation, which left Amanda in the ditch by the school, bruised and shamed once again. Her father picked her up and took her home.

With all of the emotional trauma surrounding her, and feeling as if she would never be able to get on the right track, Amanda attempted to take her own life by drinking a bottle of bleach. She was rushed to the hospital to have her stomach pumped, and after a couple days of treatment, she returned home to experience the ugliest side of social media.

Abusive messages were flowing in. "She deserved it," one status read. Another message to her read, "Have you washed the mud out of your hair yet?" Another brutal commenter wrote, "I hope she's dead. Maybe she should use a different kind of bleach next time."

> The cyber-bullying on social media did not stop, though, because despite moving physically into a new community, your online community follows you wherever you go.

Inappropriate messages and pictures lined her page for months. She eventually moved to her mother's house to try for yet another fresh start.

The cyber-bullying on social media did not stop, though, because even if you move physically into a new community, the online community follows you wherever you go. Tragically, so did the man with her photograph. This man continued to befriend those close to Amanda on social media and then distribute her photograph to as many as he could—teachers, students, administrators, etc.

Amanda began cutting herself in 2012. After counseling, an overdose, and much effort on behalf of family who loved her, Amanda posted a video recounting her experience on YouTube. This was her effort to reach out for help, while trying to inspire others to stand up to bullying. Her caption read:

> I'm struggling to stay in this world, because everything just touches me so deeply. I'm not doing this for attention. I'm doing this to be an inspiration and to show that I can be strong. I did things to myself to make pain go away, because I'd rather hurt myself then someone else. Haters are haters but please don't hate, although im sure I'll get them. I hope I can show you guys that everyone has a story, and everyones future will be bright one day, you just gotta pull through. I'm still here aren't I?[9]

Tragically, the video comments were lined with a mixture of hate and support.

On October 10, 2012, the hate got the better of Amanda, and she took her own life and was found dead in her home. She was 16 years old.

After an investigation, a man under the alias of Aydin C was charged with indecent assault and child pornography. Amanda's mother maintains the belief that more than one person was involved. Aydin C was no young boy flirting with another teen. He was a 35-year-old man.

Amanda Todd's story stands as an example of social media use gone wrong in the worst possible way. It shows the power of destructive words, even through an online medium. The "piling on" effect of social media might even be worse than other kinds of bullying. Sadly, her story is not the only one of its kind. There are many children who have taken their lives because of cyber-bullying on social media. It's a tragic use of a medium meant to bring people together.

> No online medium can diminish the power of words. In some cases it only enhances it.

A Mixed Bag

Social media truly is a mixed bag. In this chapter, I have tried to show some of the good and some of the bad. There is simply not enough space to discuss how social media has been used to topple unjust and authoritarian regimes, catch criminals, unite families, distribute helpful information, and even put a smile on most of our faces at one time or another. There are also sad stories of "digital infidelity," depression and suicide, misplaced priorities, unhealthy obsessions, comparative bitterness, and online shaming.

Social media is a place where all of these things can potentially be a part of your story. So is being connected through social media always good? Most certainly we have to say no. Is simply deciding to be disconnected the answer then? We have to say no to that question as well.

I propose there is a third way that is offered to us in Christ, "in whom are hidden all the treasures of wisdom and knowledge" (Col. 2:3). Only through the life-affirming power of the gospel can we use social media in a way that preserves its best qualities while avoiding its worst.

Reflection Questions

Which of these stories affected you the most? Why?

What are some good, bad, and ugly stories that you have heard about social media use?

What is your takeaway from these stories?

AVOIDING THE DITCHES

"He (the devil) always sends errors into the world in pairs—pairs of opposites. . . . He relies on your extra dislike of one to draw you gradually into the opposite one. But do not let us be fooled. We have to keep our eyes on the goal and go straight through between both errors. We have no other concern than that with either of them."
—C.S. Lewis

A man named Conrad Kessner took serious issue with the effects of over-connectivity and too much information on the human mind. He was so concerned about the issue that he wrote a book describing how modern technological advancements were overwhelming people with more information and data than they could handle, causing confusion and damage to the mind. More and more people share his concern about the digital sea we seem to be drowning in; after all, we are not designed to run like machines, always on. The interesting thing about Kessner is that he was a man who never used a cell phone, never logged on to Facebook, and never posted a selfie. In fact, he never even owned a computer. Before you label him as a nut, note that these things are true because he died in 1565. The ideas he shared in his book were in reference to the rise of the printing press and the seemingly unending flood of information that would result from its invention.

The observations I have made about social media technology, although somewhat unique to the medium, are not altogether new. At various times in the history of the world, societies have had to learn to cope with significant change due to innovation. In Kessler's day it was the printing press; today it's the Internet and social media.

> Even the greatest technological
> advancements bring positive and
> negative consequences.

In light of Gutenberg's invention, thousands of printed materials were being distributed across the world, and information was now more available and accessible than ever before. Works like the Bible that used to be hand-copied by monks were now being printed *en masse*. The Protestant Reformation owes much of its impact to the printing press. Between 1518 and 1520, 300,000 copies of Luther's tracts were printed and distributed. Many attribute the scientific revolution and the rise of democracy to the invention of the printing press. It was named the greatest and most influential invention of the millennium by A&E Network.

Yet people like Conrad Kessner and many others recognized the potential drawbacks of the printing press. They were misguided, right? How can you find fault with something that has such potential for good? It turns out that despite its amazing benefits, the printing press did have some drawbacks:

Roughly during the first century after Gutenberg's invention, print did as much to perpetuate blatant errors as it did to spread enlightened truth. Putting scribal products into print resulted in a cultural explosion. Never had scholars found so many words, images, and diagrams at their fingertips. And never before had things been so confusing with, for instance, Dante's worldview achieving prominent visibility at the same time that Copernican views were making their way into print. Nonsense and truth seemed to move hand in hand with neither made uncomfortable by the presence of the other. Though many have discussed Renaissance culture's playful spirit, love of many-sided accomplishment, or lighthearted indifference to historical fact, Eisenstein more prosaically says that things simply had not yet been sorted out.[1]

In other words, the rise of the printing press flooded the world with ideas, but they weren't all true. Sure, people were able to read and gain knowledge faster than ever before, but ignorance and untruth were being propagated at a faster rate, too. Famed Baptist preacher C. H. Spurgeon once quipped, "A lie will go round the world while truth is pulling its boots on."[2] Even the greatest technological advancements bring both positive and negative consequences.

Overreaction and Under-appreciation

We all know people prone to overreaction. They get in a fender-bender and then refuse to get into a car again. They get sick after eating out and swear off all restaurants. If their children get sick at a sleepover, they won't be allowed to go to one of those again. These people have difficulty seeing the proverbial "forest for the trees."

With a technological advancement like social media, it's easy to respond defensively. We feel the winds of massive change, and they can be terrifying. The knee-jerk reaction is to pull away entirely. Disconnection can seem like the only answer. Like the monks in the day of the printing press who continued to copy Scripture by hand, the temptation is to avoid change and stick with what feels familiar, safe, and comfortable.

Then there are the more laid-back types among us, happy to go with the flow and open to change. They don't get too stressed out about the holiday season. When their child gets a traffic ticket, they tend to understand. He's just a kid, right? When they get sick after eating out, they figure that at least they got to try something new. When their toddler gets sick, they view it as an opportunity to build up her immune system.

Social media doesn't concern this group nearly as much. They view it as a way to connect with others and stave off boredom. Sure, they might spend more time scrolling than they should, or their teen daughter might get a little carried away with her selfie addiction, but it really isn't that big of a deal. Just let people be connected and enjoy themselves, they figure. "Live and let live," is their motto.

We all fall somewhere on this spectrum. We can overreact to the drawbacks of social media and stay away entirely, or underestimate the pitfalls and engage uncritically and unwisely. These two responses represent ditches on either sides of the road. We tend to drift toward one or the other. The statistics and the stories we hear should make us want to avoid the ditches and find a better way to engage with wisdom.

The truth is, you aren't necessarily better off the more you connect. Connection brings with it some costs that must be considered. We can't just ignore the obvious effects social media has on our lives.

However, disconnecting altogether probably isn't the answer either for a few reasons.

Jay Jaboneta's story is just one of many stories we could have told that illustrate how social media can be used for good. Throughout my work on this project, I have talked to dozens of people who have been blessed by social media because it kept them connected with family and friends across state lines, national lines, and even oceans. And I've talked with employers who have used tools like LinkedIn to help them find quality candidates for job openings.

> Social media can be seen as a
> mission field of epic proportions.
> And if so, we must engage even if
> at great cost to ourselves.

The gospel message has gone out to countless people through social media, including some in difficult-to-reach areas. Influential godly leaders and ministers are able to distribute sermons, blogs, books, and content to a much wider audience. Pastors who may have not have had access to all the resources they need now can access more than ever before. Ministries can connect and network across great distances, increasing relational ties and making international mission work more fruitful.

Finally, with over a billion users connecting on the world's most popular social media site, it's difficult for a Christian to justify completely disconnecting from such a powerful and widespread means of communication and community. We shouldn't abandon the opportunity to engage in a community this large despite some of the possible drawbacks. Social media can be seen as a mission field of epic proportions. And if that's true, it seems we must engage at some level, even at personal cost to ourselves.

Jim Elliot, when asked why he was willing to risk his life to serve an indigenous tribe of unbelievers, said,

> Surely those who know the great passionate heart of Jehovah must deny their own loves to share in the expression of His. Consider the call from the Throne above, "Go ye," and from round about, "Come over and help us," and even the call from the damned souls below, "Send Lazarus to my brothers, that they come not to this place." Impelled, then, by these voices, I dare not stay home while Quichuas perish.[3]

I'm not equating engaging online with the sacrifice of the great missionary Jim Elliot, but there is great wisdom in his words. We should not let the drawbacks to social media overshadow the gospel need in the world around us. Social media, no matter its dangers and deficiencies, can be a powerful tool for good in the hand of a believer devoted to Christ's mission in the world.

We can't afford to be ignorant of challenges to using social media well and wisely. In fact, we must identify them and overcome them. In order to do this well, we need a tool that can help us sift through the good and bad so that we can take maximum advantage of the amazing opportunity God has given us to connect with others. In seafaring terms, we need a compass and a map to navigate the digital sea. Providentially, God has provided.

Reflection Questions

- Which of the two ditches do you tend to lean toward (all-on connectivity or all-out disconnection)? Why?

- As a Christian, do you view social media as a mission opportunity? Why or why not?

- What ways can you use social media as a force for good in your world?

PART TWO
CHARTING THE COURSE

GOSPEL GLASSES:
THE LENSES WE NEED

"I believe in Christianity as I believe that the Sun has risen, not only because I see it, but because by it I see everything else."

—C.S. Lewis

When I was 8 years old, I went to the optometrist for my first eye exam. My father and brother had perfect 20/20 vision, and my mother and sister couldn't see much of anything without corrective lenses. This left me, the fifth wheel of the family, with a 50/50 chance of needing glasses. It turned out that the elementary school nurse had tipped off my mom about my poor eyesight after a dismal showing at the yearly exam. I had to be fitted for specs.

I was a pretty awkward-looking kid already, and getting glasses probably wasn't going to help. Secretly, I really wanted them. They made you seem smart and sophisticated, at least in my severely impaired eyes. After an afternoon of dilation and tests, I was fitted with a brand new pair of prescription glasses.

Walking out of the mall that day was a new experience. Everything seemed brighter, shinier. It was almost sensory overload, as though I had been walking around my whole life in the black-and-white portion of *The Wizard of Oz* before being jolted into the living-color portion. (Unfortunately, I am color blind as well, but we will leave that portion of the story for another time.)

The experience I had with new glasses is a little like the experience the Bible says every Christian has upon conversion. Before Christ, we all looked at the world through eyes that couldn't see clearly. We only saw a blurry and distorted version of the world God had made, which left us with more questions than answers about life. Paul says that this blur and distortion is caused by a spiritual blindness being cast over us by the enemy of our souls:

> In their case the god of this world has blinded the minds of unbelievers, to keep them from seeing the light of gospel of the glory of Christ, who is the image of God (2 Cor. 4:4).

This blindness is lifted when we trust in Christ and believe the gospel.

> For God, who said 'Let light shine out of darkness' has shone in our hearts to give the light of the knowledge of the glory of God in the face of Jesus Christ (2 Cor. 4:6).

> We can't understand God, the
> world around us, or even ourselves
> without the knowledge of
> Jesus Christ.

The idea of spiritual blindness giving way to spiritual sight is not "hot of the press" stuff—it's biblical and is captured in one of the most famous hymns ever written, "Amazing Grace." The opening lines of the song are these:

Amazing grace, how sweet the sound
that saved a wretch like me.
I once was lost, but now I'm found,
was blind, but now I see [emphasis mine].

Conversion and the gift of spiritual sight happen in an instant, but have huge implications for the rest of our life and into eternity. Everything is immediately new, though learning to walk in this newness is a lifelong process of transformation.

The truth about the person and work of Jesus Christ is what brings us this sight. We can't understand God, the world around us, or even ourselves without the knowledge of Jesus Christ. When we come to understand and embrace the truth of God's redemptive plan, a veil is lifted from our eyes. Ideas about the world come into clearer focus:

Before Christ	Gospel Truth	After Christ
Things are never quite right in the world.	Sin has distorted and destroyed the world God made, and Jesus came to destroy sin.	God is restoring all things to be made well again in Christ.
My life is my own to do what I want.	My rebellion and autonomy will only lead to destruction. Jesus died to make me His own.	My life is not my own. I belong to Christ and live for His glory.
I need to make money to live out my desires.	God knows all of my needs and has provided richly in Christ.	Being commissioned by God to work, I work heartily for Him and not myself, entrusting myself wholly to Him for provision.
You only live once, so I need to live it up while I can.	Jesus died to promise eternal life to everyone who believes in Him.	Every joy and sorrow here can be leveraged to give hope and expectation for the eternal glory coming in Christ.

To know Jesus is to see the world differently. However, many of us unwisely leave our gospel glasses on the nightstand each morning before we head out the door. Having been given the gracious gift of sight, we forget to apply the truth of the gospel to everyday situations.

We make this mistake on social media most of all.

The first and most pertinent step of redeeming social media use is to approach the medium with gospel glasses on. If we are bleary-eyed and ignorant sailors of the digital sea, we are going to be buffeted by the waves and thrown off course. We need to use the greatest tool that every Christian has been given—the gospel of Jesus Christ. The gospel is the wisdom of God for us. It is only through this wisdom that we will be able to redeem this medium for God's glory.

Deconstructing and Reconstructing

Tim Keller, preaching pastor at Redeemer Church in Manhattan, has a series of lectures about sharing the gospel with a postmodern culture. In these lectures, Keller discusses how the gospel must be used as a tool to deconstruct faulty worldviews and "defeater beliefs," while simultaneously reconstructing a desirable and glorious view of the true gospel. He rightly asserts,

> People avoid Christianity, not because they have really examined its teachings and found them wanting, but because their culture gives huge plausibility (by the media, through art, through the expertise and impressive credentials of its spokespersons) to believe a series of defeater beliefs that they know are true, and since they are true, Christianity can't be.[1]

In other words, defeater beliefs are truths propped up by culture, supported through various means, pitted against gospel truth, and believed (subconsciously or consciously) by people. These beliefs effectively nullify any potential faith in Jesus because the two competing truth claims seem incompatible.

Keller says we must respond to these defeater beliefs with the gospel. Defeater beliefs are only half-truths. We must meet these half-truths with the whole truth of the gospel. Example:

Defeater Belief	Gospel Response	Half-Truth Uncovered
The Christian God seems vindictive and angry. Why does He have to kill Jesus to forgive us?	Forgiveness always requires someone to pay a price. God decided to pay the price Himself rather than require payment from us.	Even though God is angry at sin, He is not vindictive because His response to sin is the sacrifice of Jesus—God the Son.

Keller believes the gospel is the tool to deconstruct these defeater beliefs and reconstruct a true view of God and "the truth that is in Jesus" (Eph. 4:21).

The same process that Keller outlines in his talk on postmodern evangelism should be applied to the Christian's life of sanctification. We all have some defeater beliefs rattling around in our minds on a daily basis. We have not fully obtained the mind of Christ. These misbeliefs can be about God, about ourselves, or about the world around us. Whatever they are, they lead us away from truth and away from gospel faith. Any faulty belief that does not align with the truth of the gospel should be categorized as unbelief.

Simply because we have trusted Christ for salvation doesn't

mean we are immune to all error and unbelief. Remember, we still have an enemy who lies to us about what's good and true. There's also the danger of religious pride, thinking we've arrived and have things figured out. That's a dangerous place to be. Jesus diagnosed this pride in the religious elite of his day:

> If you were blind, you would have no guilt; but now that you say "We see," your guilt remains (John 9:41).

Just like the Pharisees, we often miss our own unbelief because we think we can see just fine.

We must address the possible unbelief shaping our social media engagement with gospel truth every day. We cannot accomplish this by leaving our gospel glasses on the nightstand each morning when we wake up. We must see the world through those lenses, or we are doomed to embrace untruth and walk in unbelief. Example:

Faulty Belief	Gospel Response	Half-Truth Uncovered
I am called by God to love others. I can't ignore all of these posts online by friends and family. It is unloving.	God's definition of love includes sacrifice and prioritization. Jesus even refused to heal people at one point in order to lovingly fulfill His call to the cross.	We are called to be loving, but love does not neatly fit into the category of being held emotionally hostage by myriads of online friends.

Just as Keller encourages Christians to learn the defeater beliefs of their culture so they can better share the gospel, we ought to seek to uncover the half-truths we're holding onto and replace them with gospel truth. Our lives will always go in the direction of our deepest beliefs. Kierkegaard asserts, "Our life always expresses the result of our dominant thoughts."

> We must bring our gospel glasses to the social media sphere too.

ABC's or A-Z's?

The gospel is not meant to make an appearance at the beginning of our life with Christ, never to appear again until glory. It's impossible to grow in God without a daily application of the gospel message over and over again to the heart. Keller puts it this way: "The gospel is not just the A-B-C's but the A-Z of Christianity. The gospel is not just the minimum required doctrine necessary to enter the kingdom, but the way we make progress in the kingdom."[2]

This calls for a renewed commitment to grow in grace. We cannot ignore the implications of the gospel and expect to thrive spiritually. Every Christian needs to become fluent in the gospel in a way that provides the discernment and wisdom needed to navigate the social sea in a God-glorifying way.

Reflection Questions

- Is social media an area that you find it difficult to see through the lens of the gospel? Why or why not?

- What are some "defeater" or faulty beliefs you need to fight against?

- What are the gospel truths that combat your defeater or faulty beliefs?

TIME:
THE UNBIASED COMMODITY

"The proper function of man is to live, not to exist. I shall not waste my days in trying to prolong them. I shall use my time."

—Jack London

Ancient Israel's wisest and wealthiest king, according to the Bible, was Solomon. The son of King David, Solomon was a man of great capacity and great fortune. God promised Solomon that he would be the wisest, richest, and most honored king in the history of Israel (2 Chr. 1:7–13).

The sometimes bleak but always incisive Book of Ecclesiastes, written by Solomon, begins with a consideration on the nature of time. Solomon sees the world as cyclical and seasonal. He asserts that there is a vanity to life as repeating cycles of events continue in a monotonous and never-ending fashion. He laments that some good men live and die without ever being acknowledged, while some evil men seem to live and die in comfort and ease. He follows that heavy dose of reality with the sobering truth that neither the good nor evil man knows where he is going after death, and that ultimately good men, evil men, and beasts all return to dust.

Ecclesiastes is not a chipper piece of literature.

But just like my cranky old grandfather, I think we can trust that he is telling the truth because he isn't delivering a feel-good message and has nothing to gain from lying. Solomon has gained wisdom through many hard experiences, and he's telling it like it is. Besides, God bestowed on him the title of "wisest king" (apart from Christ), so I want to lean in.

The most famous lines in Ecclesiastes are a poetic reflection on time and seasons:

> For everything there is a season, and a time for every
>   matter under heaven:
> a time to be born, and a time to die;
> a time to plant, and a time to pluck up what is planted;
> a time to kill, and a time to heal;
> a time to break down, and a time to build up;
> a time to weep, and a time to laugh;
> a time to mourn, and a time to dance;
> a time to cast away stones, and a time to gather stones
>   together;
> a time to embrace, and a time to refrain from embracing;
> a time to seek, and a time to lose;
> a time to keep, and a time to cast away;
> a time to tear, and a time to sew;
> a time to keep silence, and a time to speak;
> a time to love, and a time to hate;
> a time for war, and a time for peace (Eccles. 3:1–8.

There are times and seasons in our lives that are filled with various milestones. Birth and death, seedtime and harvest, weeping and laughing, tearing and sewing, and more. God has providentially appointed these times and seasons by His wisdom and grace.

Yet, Solomon does more than just point out God's sovereignly appointed times and seasons in our lives. He gives us a guiding principle for how to make the most of life: "I know that there is nothing better for people than to be happy and to do good while they live" (Eccles. 3:12).

Our times and seasons have been designed by God, but the wise seek to understand and *steward* these times and seasons well. They want to spend their time in a way that, in the end, doesn't induce regret.

Living wisely and well can feel like an uphill battle, as we tend to drift toward making foolish choices like most of the people around us. If we don't make a concerted, continual effort to listen to the call of wisdom, we may find ourselves experiencing a lot of regret. But it doesn't have to be that way. God freely gives wisdom to those who ask for it. And He has given us a book full of wisdom in the Bible.

Unbiased Commodity

Almost everyone has been in a situation at one time or another that's felt a little shady. Maybe you worked for a family-owned company and felt that there was some nepotism occurring there. Or perhaps you played on a team where playing time seemed to be influenced by wealthy booster club donors. Bias and unfairness are not new phenomenons; they have existed since sin entered the world. We don't live in a world of perfect justice yet.

In Genesis, Sarah favored Isaac over Ishmael; Rebekah favored Jacob over Esau; Jacob favored Joseph over his brothers. The march goes on.

> These daily decisions can seem insignificant, but they will ultimately shape the course of our lives.

Time, by contrast, is an unbiased commodity. Every single day, every person on the face of the earth is given the exact same number of seconds, minutes, and hours to utilize as they see fit. There is neither nepotism nor favoritism. The CEO of the world's largest company and the everyday blue-collar worker is given the same portion.

How we spend this commodity is mainly up to us. I think that's what Solomon was alluding to in Ecclesiastes. Every day we are faced with decisions: Should I plant or pluck up? Should I tear or sew? Should I speak or be silent? It might look like this for you:

- Should I wake up and pray or snooze for ten more minutes?

- Should I shower today or wing it with cologne?

- Should I straighten my hair or rock the ponytail?

- Should I drive or ride the bus?

- McDonalds or Chick-fil-A?

- Fries or a fruit cup?

- Lunch or a workout?

- Study or watch Netflix?

- Facebook or . . . ?

These daily decisions can seem insignificant, but they will ultimately shape the course of our lives. How we spend the seconds will define how we spend the minutes, hours, and days. The dozens of times that we check our social media accounts each day add up over the course of a week, a month, or a year. Imagine what that number could look like over a lifetime if we're not making intentional, wise choices about the time God has given us.

Stewardship

Paul tells the church at Colossae to "make the best use of the time" (Col. 4:5). In context, Paul is encouraging them to do this for the sake of advancing the gospel. Christians are called to be God's ambassadors in a world full of unbelief. Earlier in the same verse, Paul calls these unbelievers "outsiders." This term might seem a bit pretentious, but it makes sense if you think about it. Those who don't know Christ are on the outside looking in. Whether they realize it or not, making sense of the world around them is impossible apart from Christ. Everyone forms opinions, of course, but they are incomplete apart from Christ.

A Christian's life will often appear quite odd to a non-Christian. The values, dreams, hopes, and aspirations of a follower of Christ will frequently go against the grain of culture and convention, sometimes causing non-Christians to be intrigued as to why Christians make the choices they do. This creates a natural "peering in" effect as the outsider looks in to see what exactly is going on in a Christian's life to create such odd beliefs and behaviors.

> "One of the great uses of Twitter
> and Facebook will be to prove at
> the Last Day that prayerlessness
> was not from lack of time."
> —John Piper

One of the primary ways Christians should look different from the world around them is how they use their time.

With Jesus's life on the earth as our best example, we mustn't be conformed to cultural patterns in our use of the unbiased commodity of time.

In this cultural moment, there is no more pressing threat to our time than our use of social media. John Piper takes a big swing at this very real challenge to good stewardship: "One of the great uses of Twitter and Facebook will be to prove at the Last Day that prayerlessness was not from lack of time."[1]

It stings my heart to read that, but I know it's true. We are careless with the precious commodity of time that God has given to us. We tend to be busy but also wasteful. We want to know and share the latest news, often feeling a sense of urgency to stay on top of things. The wise words of fantasy author Ursula K. Le Guin come to mind: "I was in too much haste, and now have no time left."[2]

What It's Worth

My father enjoyed jewelry-making when I was a child. I remember walking into his shop on weekends and seeing him tinkering with his tools. It gave him great joy. One of my favorite things to do was to sneak into his shop and reach into a box beneath his workbench and play with his ring molds.

Ring molds are two small halves of a rectangular-shaped silicone compound used to cast metal. After the metal is hot enough and in liquid form, you pour it into the mold and let it harden. A jeweler might have thousands of different molds because there are endless jewelry designs, and not every mold is in use all the time.

I enjoyed playing with these ring molds because the silicone compound was almost like a rubber ball. I spent hours playing with them, and I destroyed dozens of them just because it was fun to break them in half and throw them around.

The first time my father caught me and realized how many I had destroyed, his face held a look of utter disbelief. These molds probably didn't cost him a fortune (although any amount would have been significant for us at that time), and the rings I ruined probably weren't of great value. But the time he had put into them, all the effort and workmanship along with the financial cost, amounted to a devastating loss. He was very upset.

Every day, many of us treat time like I treated my father's ring molds—we don't understand the true value of what's in our hands. We don't fully appreciate what we are playing around with.

The moments we waste on social media can mean little to us, but are priceless to our Father. We are like children in a craftsman's workroom, toying with the valuables. Seconds, minutes, hours, and days are shaved off our lives and left on the workroom floor as trash.

All the while, God has called us to work with Him and for Him (1 Cor. 3:9). He wants us to understand the value of our time. At some point, we must grow up, be called off the floor, and be given the tools of the workshop.

> The moments we diffuse away on
> social media mean little to us, but
> are priceless to our Father.

What Matters with Who You Love

My wife and I have different tastes in movies, to say the least. It hasn't led to too many moments of contention, but there have been a few times when we haven't seen eye-to-eye on what an ideal theater trip looks like. It isn't just individual movies that we disagree on; it's that we have different tastes in genre sometimes.

For instance, she loves romantic, time-travel movies. I know that seems incredibly specific, but there is a surprisingly robust collection of movies that fit that description. I can get into the time travel too, but her category does not include movies like *Interstellar*. We are talking a very small niche here.

So, needless to say, I have found myself sitting on the couch with my wife curled up next to me watching an inordinate number of romantic, time-travel films. Each of these movies has its own unique take on the idea, but there is one thematic similarity in every single one of them. Every person, if they had a chance to do it over again, would spend more time with the ones they love, doing the things that matter most. Even time travelers are not immune to this truth.

In my wife's favorite movie in the genre, the *crème de la crème* of time-traveler romantics, the narrative follows a young man who finds out his time-travel gift is generational.

Upon this realization, his father offers him some advice before he dies. He tells him to live each day ordinarily, as if he didn't have the ability to turn back time. Then, he should live it again a second time, "the first time with all the tensions and worries that stop us noticing how sweet the world can be, but the second time noticing."[3]

This idea of *noticing* was his term for *intentionality*. He was to spend his days doing what mattered most with the people he loved the most while not ignoring the little moments that were offered each day to do those very things. After he tries this for a while, he has an epiphany about a way to live that he believes is even better than his father's advice:

And in the end I think I've learned the final lesson from my travels in time; and I've even gone one step further than my father did: The truth is I now don't travel back at all, not even for the day, I just try to live every day as if I've deliberately come back to this one day, to enjoy it, as if it was the full final day of my extraordinary, ordinary life.[4]

Consider what kind of meaningful things that could be done with the ones we love if we approached each day with intentionality—with a kind of deliberate passion to live purposely. If there is one thing I take away from these sappy, sci-fi, romantic flicks it is that we have an opportunity each day to choose meaningfulness over meaninglessness, despite our tendency to choose the latter. Thankfully, the gospel gives us eyes to see what matters most and a heart to discern whom we ought to love the most.

Between Two Ages

When Jesus was resurrected from the dead, He gave a promise to His disciples: "I am with you always, to the end of the age" (Matt. 28:20). Christians in the early church had an understanding of time that seems largely forgotten in our day.

We are living in an age where sin remains but is slowly being redeemed by grace. Christ inaugurated His kingdom at the Resurrection, but the consummation of that kingdom has yet to be realized. Until Jesus's triumphant return, we have been commissioned to tell the world about His first coming, which will help prepare people for His second coming.

> The gospel simultaneously gives us eyes to see what matters most and a heart to discern whom we ought to love the most.

During this period before His return, Christ is redeeming and restoring the world through the ministry of the Holy Spirit working through His church. This work will not be completed until Christ's return, but it has already begun, and we are called to be involved in it.

Jesus's return will mark the beginning of a brand new age, the one we've all been looking forward to. Every saint who has ever lived has longed for this day. Faith will become sight, every tear will be wiped away, and the Lamb will be King of His new city forever.

Apart from the glorious vanquishment of all sin and

suffering, there is another stark difference between the current age and the one to come. The age to come will never end. Time is limitless there because it is eternal. Our current age has a time clock on it. None of us know how long until the clock stops, but we know we are on a countdown.

This knowledge drove the early church to view time differently. They understood that time is limited, and they knew that it should be used wisely for the King's glory.

The irony here is that this is true for us also, even if Jesus doesn't return in our lifetime. To use Solomon's words, there is "a time to be born, and a time to die." We are all on a time clock, but we don't know how much time we have left. So it is all the more imperative that we carefully steward our time in the best possible ways.

An Unrealistic Proposal

I'm not naïve; to expect an immediate, 180-degree shift in time-management habits in the area of online use seems a little unrealistic. Nonetheless, the gospel does produce radical change in those fully submitted to God, and it creates followers whose obedience is out of step with the rest of society. I propose that an "unrealistic" redistribution of how we spend our time is in order for many of us.

> We are all on a time clock, but we don't know how much time we have left.

What's at stake? If we don't get serious about walking in wisdom here, we are going to tweet and Snapchat our way into eternity with perhaps only some cute status updates and well lighted selfies to show for far too much of our time. Our children might grow up with parents more distracted and less gospel-focused than they could and should have been. We might neglect the call to love our neighbors by getting to know them personally and sharing the gospel with them as we have opportunity. Our spouses could miss out on our being fully present with them. These aren't absolutes, but they are possibilities, and in some cases, probabilities. So what is my unrealistic proposal?

Absolutely refuse to allow Facebook and Twitter feeds, Instagram comments, or Snapchat stories take up the bulk of your free time. Make that commitment to God and yourself. I know we're all looking for the next time-management technique that miraculously sets us free from distraction and keeps us focused. Let me lovingly suggest that there is no secret technique that will make this process easy. We have to own the problem ourselves. And in some cases, we might have to radically restructure how we use our time.

Having said all that, I have some great news. Jesus is ready to help us. He is willing and able to guide us along wise paths of stewardship, leading to the joy and peace we long for. In fact, He desires that for us far more than we desire it for ourselves. What can seem like a path of denial and deprivation is truly the path to a richer and fuller life. That's exactly what Jesus came to give us (John 10:10). Will you trust Him with your time?

Reflection Questions

When, where, and why do I most often use social media?

How can I restructure my day to help better utilize my time?

Are there any wise boundaries I could set in place that would help me better steward my time (e.g., no phones in bedroom, no phones at dinner, etc.)?

SPEECH:
THE RUDDER OF THE SHIP

"What comes out of the mouth proceeds from the heart, and this defiles a person."

—Jesus

"Sweetheart, you have a voice that carries." My first-grade teacher, Mrs. Walker, had a penchant for euphemisms. I was your typical overly excited, loud kid. My full-on rebellious behavioral issues did not emerge until second grade, but poor Mrs. Walker had to deal with my loud voice in class from day one.

It, or *I*, was an all-day affair for her. During flashcard time, I shouted the answer loudly and before anyone else could even look at the card. During library question-and-answer time, I answered every question without raising my hand. No matter the activity, no matter the subject, I shouted out the answer loudest and first. It didn't matter that I was right most of the time. For a first-grade teacher trying to teach an entire class, I was a nightmare.

My boisterousness has been an issue since I was young, but I didn't quite know the extent of it until I was married.

I remember the first time my wife came to me and graciously said, "I hate it when you interrupt me. I can never finish a sentence without you talking over me." I felt as if I had walked headfirst into a brick wall. I was a little stunned.

Here's the thing: I genuinely didn't know the extent of my rudeness. I'm not saying I was walking around with no regard for human life, constantly yelling. Don't picture that guy. But I could be unintentionally obnoxious, and I was lacking in some self-awareness. (I'm still a work in progress, by the way.)

Anyway, when my mind is engaged in a conversation, my mouth tends to move ahead of the dialogue. I'm jumping steps ahead and making conclusions while others are still formulating their sentences. It doesn't help that my voice is stronger than most, and that whispering is not one of my top-ten gifts (or even bottom-ten, for that matter). I struggle with "thinking out loud" too often in a conversation. Perhaps because nothing engages me more than the hearty exchange of ideas.

Mrs. Walker knew something about me before I was even able to read. She knew I had a speech problem despite being a well above average reader and speaker. My speech problem wasn't a head issue; my speech problem was a heart issue.

Loud and Unclear

Our culture has a speech problem too. No, I'm not referring to the possible erosion of the First Amendment and our freedom of speech. I'm grateful for the level of freedom we still enjoy. The speech problem I'm talking about looks a lot like my speech problem in first grade. We are loud, we talk without thinking, and we don't understand why everyone else won't just shut up and listen to us.

This was my struggle as a young boy. It was hard to have to sit in a corner and not engage in dialogue with the class, simply because I was right and no one would listen to me. I couldn't understand why I was being punished for being good at school and having the right answers. Pride starts early. I'm a case study in it.

Social media has fueled the fire for a culture that embodies my first-grade self. If you were to scroll down your newsfeed right now, you could probably pick out several examples of what I'm talking about. Too many words; not enough listening.

> We are loud, we talk without thinking, and we don't understand why everyone else won't just shut up and listen to us.

Included among this group are the people who tend to use social media to "live-tweet" what's happening somewhere or anywhere. These "live-tweeters" offer up their ongoing inner dialogue about their life or an event as it unfolds. It's not that their information is always wrong or uninteresting; it's that it tends to include a lot of unnecessary and self-indulgent material too. They say too much, too often.

Megaphones and Ink Pens

Joe was a successful, solid guy who made a good impression on most everyone he met. He was a college graduate who spent time interning at a local tech company for a year and was now looking for a full-time position at a new start-up.

The company was young and thriving. Joe knew that if he could just get his foot in the door, he could make an impact there and make progress toward his goals. His first and second interviews had gone well, as expected. It seemed like Joe was a shoo-in for the position, and he felt confident that he could do the job well if given the opportunity.

As he sat in front of the Board of Directors for his final interview, he felt a tension in the room. They had just heaped praise on him for his competency in the field and for his score on the company chemistry assessment. He couldn't figure out the disappointment on their faces.

"We would love to offer you this position, Joe. We just aren't sure that you are the right fit for our company."

Joe was shocked. "I respect your decision, of course, but if you don't mind me asking, in what ways am I not a good fit? I mean, I feel confident in my performance evaluations and core competencies."

"We all agree, Joe, and everything checked out except for one thing. We're concerned about your judgment in some areas, and we can't afford to take a chance with this position. We are sorry."

Joe seemed to have everything going for him, but he had one strike against him. The HR Team had done some background work, as they do with all of their candidates. Joe had had a strong social media presence in college and was still very active online. With tons of friends and followers on social media, he was a very popular and outspoken guy, much like he was in person.

The problem was that Joe showed some of the same symptoms online that I had shown in Mrs. Walker's class. He had a history of making unwise and unfiltered comments. This wasn't just a couple of misguided moments of indiscretion followed by rapid apologies for stepping out of line. This was a habit of quick, inconsiderate speech, and it cost Joe a job opportunity.

There was a time when a guy like Joe would have gotten that job without question. I mean, he was a "can't miss" hire. He still might have been prone to say things he shouldn't, but it probably would have taken people a while to notice, and the consequences likely wouldn't have been as severe. But now, in a world with social media, what used to be said to a few is shouted from a megaphone to many, and what used to be written in pencil is written in ink.

My parents used to tell me, "If you want to get a tattoo, you better like it. You don't get a do-over."

> But now, what used to be said to a few is shouted from a megaphone, and what used to be written in pencil is written in ink.

Social media creates a slew of tattoos—each as permanent as the last. And each one isn't just a personal message that can be hidden, but is openly portrayed for all the world to see. The reality is that others can and will judge our character based on our words, so we must use good judgment at all times.

Thankfully, the Scriptures give us some guidance about how to approach the megaphone-and-ink world of social media: "When words are many, transgression is not lacking, but whoever restrains his lips is prudent" (Prov. 10:19).

The Allure of Controversy

It's easy to see how the combination of social media and our fast-paced culture is little like a gas leak near a foundry—explosive. It can look like a crowd of people shouting their opinions at the top of their lungs all in one place, expecting everyone to listen and respond.

Your newsfeeds can be littered with controversy. Political views, religious views, global conflicts, and relational squabbles closer to home frequently make up a significant portion of online content. Trolls have their unwelcome place in this environment too, but sometimes it's just regular people who are embroiled in the controversy.

How does this happen? Well, sin and self-righteousness is certainly partly to blame. The book of James gives us a helpful corrective: "Know this my beloved brothers: let every person be quick to hear, slow to speak, slow to anger" (James 1:19).

Sadly, we often practice the opposite. We are quick to speak, quick to anger, and slow to hear. We often fail to listen to the whole story before we comment on it. We rarely open our ears before our mouths. We speak loudly and rashly before thinking, and we are angered because others do the same. Social media can be a breeding ground for quick, opinionated barbs and passive-aggressive jabs. Apart from awareness and God's help, we will fail to apply James's wisdom online.

> We are quick to speak, quick to anger, and slow to hear.

It just doesn't take much to get our gears turning. And once we get worked up about something, it can be hard to settle back down. Pride and self-righteousness run deep. That's why we so badly need the grace of God in this area.

Despite what we've been saying, some of us might feel pretty good about ourselves because we've generally shown self-control on social media, especially compared to other people we know. The thing is, we don't have to broadcast inappropriate speech on social media for it to be wrong. Complaining to friends and family can be just as bad. Jesus said, "Therefore whatever you have said in the dark shall be heard in the light, and what you have whispered in private rooms shall be proclaimed on the housetops" (Luke 12:3).

We all need to watch our words. Our speech can so easily betray us, which is why James compares it to a beast that must be tamed. I learned this in first grade, and I will tell you now that nothing is more difficult for me than taming my words. Too often I say what I shouldn't say and don't say what I should say. And I'm a pastor!

James puts it far better than I could:

Not many of you should become teachers, my brothers, for you know that we who teach will be judged with greater strictness. For all stumble in many ways. And if anyone does not stumble in what he says, he is a perfect man, able also to bridle his whole body. If we put bits into the mouths of horses so that they obey us, we guide their whole bodies as well. Look at the ships also: though they are so large and are driven by strong winds, they are guided by a very small rudder wherever the will of the pilot directs. So also the tongue is a small member, yet it boasts of great things.

How great a forest is set ablaze by such a small fire! And the tongue is a fire, a world of unrighteousness. The tongue is set among our members, staining the whole body, setting on fire the entire course of life, and set on fire by hell. For every kind of beast and bird, of reptile and sea creature, can be tamed and has been tamed by mankind, but no human being can tame the tongue. It is a restless evil, full of deadly poison. With it we bless our Lord and Father, and with it we curse people who are made in the likeness of God. From the same mouth come blessing and cursing. My brothers, these things ought not to be so. Does a spring pour forth from the same opening both fresh and salt water? Can a fig tree, my brothers, bear olives, or a grapevine produce figs? Neither can a salt pond yield fresh water (James 3:1–12).

There are very few passages of Scripture that are more convicting to me than that one. It's as though James has been reading my journal. First, he says that teachers, like me, are held to a higher standard. Then he goes on to say that we all *stumble* in our words. Despite our culture of "speak your mind," there is such a thing as saying the wrong thing, and we all do it sometimes.

The political climate we're in highlights this reality. Any offhanded comment by a candidate can become headline news in minutes. It can turn the tide of an entire election.

James's words are so crucial for our time: What we say online can be like pouring gasoline or water on a fire. We can be arsonists or firefighters with our words. And like the rudder of a ship or the bridle in a horse's mouth, it determines our direction. Our words flow from our hearts.

Taming the tongue is the first step toward taming our entire person.

We know that in Christ we have been given a pure fountain of living water (John 4). Our source is clear as crystal, yet often our words are dark and muddy. James says we curse and speak death with the same mouth that sings praises to the Savior who became a curse for us, and that just isn't right. James calls us on our hypocrisy.

Many of us wrongly believe that our online status updates and comments are somehow disconnected from our everyday speech. This is wishful thinking. What we say online and what we say in person are no different. We need to understand that. We aren't given a free pass to say whatever we want online simply because we aren't confronted with the immediate consequences of social exclusion and individual confrontation. Instead, we are called to approach our online speech with the same care as our face-to-face interactions.

The Controlling Voice

In the beginning, the serpent used words to deceive Adam and Eve into disobeying God's command. It's interesting because not only did he deceive with words, but his prevailing argument was against the truthfulness of God's Word:

Did God actually say you shall not eat of any tree in the garden? (Gen. 3:1).

His question challenged what God had told them. It was an assault against the reliability and goodness of the words God spoke that caused the original Fall.

Jesus defeated the devil in an epic standoff in the desert. Satan, as he is wont to do, attacked the very words of God. He tried to convince Jesus to throw Himself off the temple so that the angels would rescue Him and prove His identity as the Son of God.

Jesus wasn't fooled for a second. He understood that Satan commonly misused the Word of God to deceive others. Instead, Jesus rightly used God's Word to diffuse Satan's attack.

We are in a similar battle daily. There are competing voices in our lives that vie for our attention. We must decide whether we will be listen to our own inner dialogue, the sly words of the serpent, or the loving voice of Christ. Which voice will be the rudder of our ship?

- Will we respond with anger to hasty remarks made online, or will we respond with the grace and patience of Jesus?

- Will we respond quickly to cultural issues with very little effort given to really trying to listen and understand, or will we follow the advice of James and the example of our Savior and be slow to speak?

- Will we react to the latest news cycle with our own "hot take" opinion, or will we be wise and "slow to anger," choosing instead to be silent at times as our wise Savior was sometimes silent?

These are the important questions that we're faced with daily.

Paul gives us some gospel guidance to keep in mind when we're tempted to just react based on our feelings: "For the love of Christ controls us, for we have concluded this: one has died for all, therefore all have died" (2 Cor. 5:14).

Here, Paul gives us the answer to our struggle with speech. The love displayed in the death of Jesus should control our words. We're not only thankful for His death, but by faith we have symbolically joined Him in His death. And dead people don't respond angrily to things that aren't that important. If our old self is truly dead in Christ, our online speech should look drastically different from the rest of the world. Our reactions should never be impatient and unkind. Dead people just don't get that riled up about things.

> It is the love of Christ that becomes the controlling voice in our lives— the rudder of our ship.

It is the love of Christ that becomes the controlling voice in our lives—the rudder of our ship. Rather than trying to say something to plead our case, we are content with our identity being hidden in the One who has won our case for us. As we meditate on the love displayed for us at Calvary, let us become vessels of that same love with the sharpness of our speech blunted, and the anger in our hearts calmed. Then we can use our "voice that carries" to proclaim a message worth hearing.

Reflection Questions

If someone were to do a study of your social media status updates and comments, what might they learn about your life?

Are there things that you regret saying in light of the gospel call for patience and kindness in speech and all things?

How can you move forward and use social media to speak life and encouragement into others?

Are you prone to making a lot of mistakes on social media? Consider asking someone you trust to hold you accountable for the tone and content of things you post. Give them permission to speak truth into your life.

SILENCE:
THE WIND IN THE SAIL

"In the silence of the heart God speaks. If you face God in prayer and silence, God will speak to you. Then you will know that you are nothing. It is only when you realize your nothingness, your emptiness, that God can fill you with Himself. Souls of prayer are souls of great silence."

—Mother Theresa

Sedatephobia[1] is the coined term by psychologists for the fear of silence. This diagnosis was basically unheard of half a century ago, but has steadily risen to prominence in the modern age. For sedatephobics, periods of silence can lead to high anxiety or even panic attacks.

One of the greatest fears for a sedatephobic is a power outage. Without electricity there are fewer opportunities for comfort noise. Computers, televisions, radios, and even Wi-Fi are unavailable in a power outage, which can create high levels of anxiety for the sedatephobic.

Unsurprisingly, most experts have linked the rise of sedatephobia to the increasing noise that technology brings. Most human beings just don't experience much silence anymore. From streaming music to TV to traffic, there's hardly a quiet moment in our lives. The fear of silence has to be one of the defining characteristics of our age.

The Loss of Silence

As Andrew Sullivan's story in chapter 2 showed, we are a culture largely devoid of peace and quiet. The technological revolution has made it possible for us to never have to sit and be silent. We're used to it that way. I'm a case in point.

I wake up, turn over, and check my phone. After rolling over to set my feet on the floor, I often turn on some music or audio of some sort as I dress and have breakfast. As I jump in my car, I either plug in my phone or turn on sports radio for the drive into work. Once at my desk, I flip on my computer and stream some music or a podcast as I answer emails. Throughout the day, apart from little moments of interaction or meetings, I'm pretty much listening to something.

And it doesn't have to be sound for it to be noisy. Our internal lives are busy too. The busyness and hurriedness of our culture drives up the inner volume to uncomfortable levels. At my desk, I could be listening to nothing at all, but my email inbox is still clamoring for attention, my phone is buzzing with new messages, and the little icon for my social media accounts shows that I have alerts.

Alerts. I find this to be a painfully accurate description of how they operate. Social media has a way of installing an internal alarm system in us that goes off periodically throughout the day. These alarms and alerts jolt us out of whatever we were doing and remind us that there are thousands of people waiting to hear from us online. We have new messages to respond to, new comments to like, new pictures to favorite, new storylines to follow, and new information to consume. These alerts buzz their way into our lives and create a noisy, distraction-filled reality that never slows down. Sullivan astutely diagnosed the final straw that broke silence's back:

> The smartphone revolution of the past decade can be seen in some ways simply as the final twist of [the] ratchet, in which those few remaining redoubts of quiet—the tiny cracks of inactivity in our lives—are being methodically filled with more stimulus and noise.[2]

So even when we are given opportunities for silence, we tend to reject them. Accepting moments of silence means rejecting connectivity, and we have deemed that a negative thing. We are a culture of "get it done" and "make it happen," and things don't get done or happen without busyness, noise, and connectivity.

> Accepting moments of silence
> means rejecting connectivity,
> and we have deemed that
> a negative thing.

Perhaps it's because we attach a certain level of cordiality to being available to others, or it might be that we simply enjoy the entertainment value of connectivity more than we desire silence. Whatever the reasons, silence has been lost in our lives, and we need to get it back.

The Anatomy of Quiet

Saints of old understood the need for quiet. King David famously said, "Be still before the Lord and wait patiently for him" (Ps. 37:7). His son Solomon also knew the foolishness of constant busyness and noise: "Better is a handful of quietness than two handfuls of toil and striving after wind" (Eccles. 4:6).

Jesus often withdrew to a desolate place for solitude and prayer. Even in His day, there was plenty of clamoring and noise to distract the soul.

God has woven into the fabric of creation a thread of rest. In the giving of the Law, He commanded Israel to take one day a week as a Sabbath. This day was to be wholly consecrated to the Lord through solemn rest. It was not a new idea given to Moses by God at Sinai, but an ingredient of our design going back to Genesis. In the beginning, God worked 6 days to create the world, and He rested on the seventh. Since God is omnipotent and does not grow tired, we can conclude that He rested for our sake. He established a rhythm of rest for us.

> Silence encourages the mental, physical, spiritual, and emotional rest that is required for fruitful labor. Without it, we are constantly running on fumes.

There is an inextricable link between rest and renewal. Each night we lie down to sleep and wake up renewed with strength and vigor. When we don't get enough sleep, we don't function well. We are made to rest. Even our brains are hardwired for it. As the day wanes and the sun sets, our bodies release chemicals that cause drowsiness and help us fall asleep.

It's no coincidence that there's a quiet peacefulness about the nighttime. Silence encourages rest and in turn revives the human spirit. Silence encourages the mental, physical, spiritual, and emotional rest that is required for fruitful labor. Without it, we are constantly running on fumes.

Silence also allows for helpful contemplation. When our minds aren't constantly engaged with entertainment, information, or work, our thoughts begin to drift toward the things that matter most. Silence allows us to turn down all of the competing voices in our life and turn up the volume of the Holy Spirit. Often, when we're busy with distractions and too much internal noise, what we need most is the calming effect of silence to allow clarity and wisdom to come into our hearts. This issue with distraction and avoiding silence is not unique to our generation. Spurgeon laments the distraction of his day:

> There are times when solitude is better than society, and silence is wiser than speech. We should be better Christians if we were more alone, waiting upon God, and gathering through meditation on His Word spiritual strength for labour in his service. We ought to muse upon the things of God, because we thus get the real nutriment out of them. . . . Why is it that some Christians, although they hear many sermons, make but slow advances in the divine life? Because they neglect their closets, and do not thoughtfully meditate on God's Word. They love the wheat, but they do not grind it; they would have the corn, but they will not go forth into

the fields to gather it; the fruit hangs upon the tree, but they will not pluck it; the water flows at their feet, but they will not stoop to drink it. From such folly deliver us, O Lord.[3]

Pascal's view of the importance of silence was even more pronounced: he thought our tendency for evil and disobedience were a direct result of our inability to sit quietly in silence. "All of humanity's problems stem from man's inability to sit quietly in a room alone," he wrote.[4]

Pascal said that we distract ourselves in order to keep ourselves from experiencing the uncomfortable feelings that silence can bring. When we sit in silence, we are forced to grapple with deep heart desires and soul-wearying frustrations. And yet, there is a profound healthiness to be gained by sitting quietly before the Lord. Time spent with Him gives us healing and insight that we can receive in no other way.

> "All of humanity's problems stem from man's inability to sit quietly in a room alone."

Two Dumb Men

Nebuchadnezzar was a king of high royal standing. He ruled over the city of Babylon and over the people of Israel whom God had sent into exile. The Bible records that Nebuchadnezzar was a man who had dreams and visions from the Lord. He had seen God's power at work in his city. He knew that the Lord was truly the King of heaven and earth. Yet Nebuchadnezzar's pride was great.

One day as he was walking on the roof of his royal palace, he began to talk to himself, saying,

> Is not this great Babylon, which I have built by my mighty power as a royal residence and for the glory of my majesty? (Dan. 4:30).

This was the beginning of a significant moment in Nebuchadnezzar's life. As he was still speaking, a voice from heaven fell and said,

> O King Nebuchadnezzar, to you it is spoken: The kingdom has departed from you, and you shall be driven from among men, and your dwelling shall be with the beasts of the field. And you shall be made to eat grass like an ox, and seven periods of time shall pass over you, until you know that the Most High rules the kingdoms of men and gives it to whom he will (Dan. 4:31–32).

Although this is one of the more fantastical stories in Scripture, the Bible records that Nebuchadnezzar actually experienced exactly what God decreed. He was humiliated, struck dumb, and sent away into the fields as a beast for 7 years.

Zechariah was a priest of God in the days preceding Jesus's birth. He and his wife had longed for a child but had never been able to conceive. By the providence of God, he was chosen by lot to burn incense before the Lord one day. As the people of the town waited outside, the angel Gabriel appeared before Zechariah as he performed the ritual ceremony. Gabriel brought incredible news to Zechariah of a son who would be born to him and his wife Elizabeth. This son was to be named John.

Zechariah didn't believe him. Elizabeth was old. He was old. The likelihood of birth was slim to none. Gabriel's response to Zechariah sounds familiar:

> I am Gabriel. I stand in the presence of God, and I was sent to bring you this good news. And behold, you will be silent and unable to speak until the day that these things take place, because you did not believe my words, which will be fulfilled in their time (Luke 1:19–20).

Zechariah is struck mute from that day until John's birth.

Both of these men, Nebuchadnezzar and Zechariah, experienced a silencing from God. One was a Jew, the other a Gentile. One a king, the other a lowly priest. One was wealthy, the other not. One was a follower of Yahweh, the other a pagan. But both experienced something startlingly similar and each for similar reasons.

Each of these two men struggled embracing the sovereignty of God. They struggled to believe that God governs the entire universe, and that He alone directs the affairs of all nations and people. Nebuchadnezzar and Zechariah said two totally different things, but their hearts were similar in their unbelief.

Nebuchadnezzar pridefully placed himself at the center of the universe. He foolishly imagined that he alone could build something as glorious as Babylon, and he loved himself for it.

Zechariah functionally operated in a similar way—out of

unbelief. He was a lowly priest who couldn't have children. He thought God either couldn't or wouldn't reach down and change the trajectory of his family's life. It didn't matter that Zechariah was doing a religious act in the midst of a religious people with a religious role and responsibility when confronted by Gabriel. He was still functionally operating out of unbelief, viewing himself as the god of his own family. That's why Gabriel had to remind Zechariah that he represented Almighty God, the One capable of doing anything, including giving Zechariah a son.

We ought to see ourselves in these men's stories. Much of our online addiction and our aversion to silence is due to our struggle with the sovereignty of God. We have a hard time believing that God is actually governing the entire universe. Our fear of missing out (FOMO) is simply unbelief. We weren't created to be "in" on everything happening in the world. We weren't meant to carry the load of thousands of cyber-relationships.

It's God's job to run the universe, and He does it very well. He knows the intricate details of our lives and is able to reach into those details according to His own goodness, wisdom, and love to do far more than we can fathom, despite our unbelief.

God's response to these two men gives us insight into the healing nature of silence. He consigns them both to long periods of silence and humbling. This is a cosmic time-out. God wants both of these men to take a long, hard look in the mirror and be reminded of their smallness. They need to understand their relative powerlessness in the grand scheme of things.

Social media often scratches the ancient itch we all have to "be like God." This was Nebuchadnezzar's *overt* sin and

Zechariah's *covert* sin. Nebuchadnezzar thought he was omnipotent over the nations; Zechariah doubted God's omnipotence over his own family. Both were living from a place of unbelief.

We want to be omniscient, and social media leads us to believe that we can know everything important about everyone important in our lives. Social media whispers to us that all of the pertinent information about others is right there at our fingertips.

We want to be omnipresent too. We know we can't break the third dimension, but social media seems to come close. And because we can virtually be just about anywhere on our phones, we are rarely anywhere in real life. We struggle to be present in the here and now.

And, finally, we want to feel omnipotent. Somehow we believe that if we're connected to everyone we love, then perhaps harm won't befall them. Or, if it does, we'll be right there to come to the rescue. That's why we feel anxious when we're apart from our phones for very long or when our Wi-Fi connection is out. These interruptions challenge the illusions we're living by and cause us to get anxious and angry.

Silence has a way of humbling us and getting us in touch with reality. Social media allows us to be so constantly engaged that we start to think we are essential to the management of the universe. We have a tendency to think of ourselves more highly than we ought, and noise and busyness have a way of distracting us from the truth. Silence before God reminds us that we are most definitely not Him, and we're actually glad to rediscover that fact.

Holy Hush

Picture yourself standing at the mouth of the Grand Canyon. Depth and width of breathtaking proportions stretch out before you in a reddish glow. In those moments of awe, breaking the silence can feel disrespectful. Silence is the only appropriate response to the grandeur before you.

I remember my first trip to St. Paul's Cathedral in London. Inside the front doors, there's a hush that falls upon every person. All of the hustle and bustle of tourism slows down to a crawl in this place, even in a city as unrelentingly busy as London. There is a sacredness permeating the walls and staircases—a holy hush surrounds everything.

This kind of experience is available to the Christian every day. We can sit silently before the grandeur and sacredness of Almighty God, listening only to Him. By taking a seat before Him, we humble ourselves and accept that our place in the world is not to rule but to worship. We're not kings ourselves but subjects of a good and wise King. We're not meant to know as much as we can about everyone and everything. Yet we serve a God who does know about everyone and everything, and He has the ability to reach into our everyday lives to bless us as he did Zechariah and Elizabeth.

> Silently meditating on the truth of the gospel will produce increasing levels of humility, gratitude, and wonder in us.

This is the beauty of the incarnation. The grandeur and reliability of God come together in the person of Jesus. God announced His arrival through a cosmic, angelic performance. But notice who the audience was: a group of lowly shepherds. Everything about the incarnation is filled with paradox, including the King of the universe being born in a measly manger. This King ushered in a kingdom where the values of this world are turned upside-down—or, really, right-side up for the first time. Silently meditating on the truths of the gospel will produce increasing levels of humility, gratitude, and wonder in us.

In a world that rejects silence, we ought to embrace it as a gift. When we make room for silence in our lives, we allow the wind of God's Spirit to propel us into an online world that needs to be engaged with the loving grace of the gospel. But if we aren't faithful to step away and listen to our Heavenly Father, what could we possibly offer to this noisy and busy world except more noise?

Reflection Questions

How often do you find yourself listening to someone or something vs. sitting in silence? Is it difficult for you to sit in silence? Why or why not?

What are some ways you can create times of silence in your family to enjoy God's presence?

What are some obstacles to silence that could potentially frustrate these plans? How can you overcome these obstacles?

SELF:
THE MIRROR WE MADE

"This is gospel-humility, blessed self-forgetfulness. Not thinking less of myself as in modern cultures, or less of myself as in traditional cultures. Simply thinking of myself less."

—Tim Keller

The young boy Narcissus was beautifully handsome and loved by many, but Narcissus loved only himself. The story goes that the young man was cursed one day by the goddess Aphrodite after scorning the love of a young woman named Echo. Her unrequited love toward Narcissus angered Aphrodite. His rejection of Echo was a rejection of love itself. And since Narcissus only seemed to truly love himself, Aphrodite seized an opportunity to destroy him.

One day, tired after a long day of hunting, Narcissus knelt down near a pool of clear water, thirsty for a drink. To his surprise, he was met with a beautiful face staring back up at him from the clear glass of the cool water. As soon as he saw it, he fell in love. This love was a madness that he could not control. He could think of nothing else. "Beautiful water nymph. Be mine! I love you!" he cried.

Desperately he plunged his arms into the water to grab the face of the one he loved, but as soon as his hands touched the surface, the face vanished, leaving him to grasp only pebbles at the bottom of the pool. Narcissus peered intently at the water, concerned that perhaps he had chased the beautiful one away. But soon, the face appeared again as the water stilled.

Aphrodite had kept Narcissus from knowing the truth. He saw only his own reflection and could never experience anything but unrequited love for it. He was bound to experience the same kind of rejection that he had given to Echo.

Narcissus was so enchanted by what he saw that he stayed by the pool day and night, gazing into the beautiful eyes that looked back at him. And there, by the pool, he died, and the beautiful face disappeared with him.

Creating Projections

The term narcissism, or the excessive love of self, was coined by Sigmund Freud in light of the myth of Narcissus. There are numerous studies correlating classic narcissism and social media usage. Most of these studies provide no insight into the chicken-or-the-egg conundrum. In other words, are we narcissists by nature who found an outlet in social media? Or, is social media a kind of generator of narcissism? Researchers aren't sure.

Both might be true.

What we can say is that the myth of Narcissus can provide insights into our social media use.

Social media allows us to create projections of ourselves online. We get to develop our identity from scratch by creating an online profile. We know better than to create to a complete fantasy because our real-life friends might call us on it. Nonetheless, these projections of ourselves can serve as mirrors for us to gaze into daily.

> Every picture or status we post becomes another slightly different angle to view ourselves from.

Every picture or status we post becomes another slightly different angle to view ourselves from. Much like Narcissus, we soon fall in love with our own image, and our social media profiles reflect back this love of ourselves.

Before too long, these projections can represent a great deal of our identity. Our self-love hits Narcissus-level importance to us as we check our projection moment-by-moment to see if others have heaped as much praise our way as we feel is due to us. We long for their likes, favorites, comments, and retweets because they further the story we've been telling ourselves. They assure us that others think our projections are as beautiful as we think they are.

Perhaps it's more than coincidental that Narcissus died peering into the dimly lit reflection pool, and we are slowly dying as we do the same. A light glow on our faces at the bus stop, the grocery store, the dining room table, church, the coffee shop, and our living rooms every day reveals the narcissism that lives in us all.

The Love of Self vs. The Love of God

The Scriptures answer the chicken-and-the-egg argument for us in a way that statistical analysis can't. Narcissism wasn't born from social media, but social media shines a bright light on our heart's tendency for self-absorption. Sin is at the bottom of our inordinate self-love.

The apostle Paul believed wholeheartedly that the days between Jesus's ascension and His eventual return would be marked by out-of-control self-love:

> But understand this, in the last days there will come times of difficulty. For people will be lovers of self (2 Tim. 3:1–2).

That's only the first in a long list of sinful attitudes and behaviors that Paul said would characterize the last days. The fact that he mentions it first is probably no coincidence since inappropriate self-love can lead to all kinds of darkness.

Inordinate, *selfish* self-love is the very antithesis of God's love. (There is such thing as a type of godly self-love and self-acceptance that is produced as we root our identity in light of God's love and acceptance of us through the gospel. That's not what we're talking about here, though.) God, in His infinite perfection, chose to create the entire universe out of selfless love. The Bible is chock-full of examples of His selfless love:

- God lovingly rescues Noah from the flood.
- God graciously provides Abraham an heir.
- God mercifully redeems Israel from her slave masters.

- God continually restores Israel from her oppressors.
- God allows Israel to appoint a king, despite their willful and offensive rejection of Him as King.

We could easily keep going. God is extremely others-focused in the Scriptures. Only God's love can break the bonds of narcissism. He is worthy of our worship. His name and renown will one day be the eternal song of the nations. Yet we live in a world where

- God is not acknowledged
- God is not praised
- God is mocked and ridiculed
- God is hated and despised
- Obedience to God is seen as outdated or ridiculous
- Evil is celebrated and lauded as good
- Jesus's sacrifice is touted as divine child abuse
- The Holy Spirit is grieved and widely quenched
- Some have declared themselves to be their own god
- Others have fashioned new gods to suit their desires

Only God's great love and patience prevents this world from complete disintegration due to foolishness and selfishness. Thank God His love is not like ours!

"The love of God is like himself—equal, constant, not capable of augmentation or diminution; our love is like ourselves—unequal, increasing, waning, growing, declining. His, like the sun, always the same in its light, though a cloud may sometimes interpose; ours, as the moon, has its enlargements and straightenings."[1]

—John Owen

God's amazing love is sustaining this broken, fallen world moment-by-moment, despite our destructive tendency to worship ourselves.

The Cross and Death to Self

The selfless love of Jesus Christ stands in stark contrast to our narcissistic habit of focusing way too much on ourselves. There is no greater example of God's selfless love than the cross of Christ.

For God so loved the world that he gave his only begotten Son, that whoever believes in him will not perish but inherit eternal life (John 3:16).

As our selfie-laden culture clamors for a small piece of online glory, Jesus shows us a different and better way. His head hangs low, crowned with thorns as He drags the cross to Calvary's hill. Here the Christian road diverts from every other path. We must decide if we will follow the Lamb of God outside the camp, or if we will fall in line with the crowds and continue our pursuit of self-love.

The New Testament is not difficult to interpret on this subject. Commentators don't really argue over the meaning of following Jesus. The call to follow Him is a call to die to yourself. Paul said it like this:

We were buried therefore with him by baptism into death, in order that, just as Christ was raised from the dead by the glory of the Father, we too might walk in newness of life (Rom. 6:4).

So you also must consider yourself dead to sin and alive to God in Christ Jesus (Rom. 6:11).

I have been crucified with Christ. It is no longer I who live, but Christ who lives in me (Gal. 2:20).

These are just a few of the New Testament's many references to self-denial and death to self. Jesus's words were even more pointed:

If anyone would come after me, let him deny himself and take up his cross and follow me (Matt. 16:24).

According to Jesus, a prerequisite for discipleship is self-denial.

Social media not only allows us to toe the line of self-love and reject the narrow way of the Savior, it threatens to redefine the line altogether. Self-promotion is so common that it almost sounds restrictive and unnecessary to question it. I can almost hear the dissenters: "Why are you trying to silence people's passion? Everyone should be allowed to express themselves!"

I understand that sentiment, but freedom of speech and expression is different from self-exaltation, and we must be careful not to redefine one or the other. We fall into the trap of self-exaltation because narcissism, not selflessness, is our natural bent. That's why Jesus challenges our self-focus, calling us to instead focus on following Him.

The Other Way

The way of the cross offers a different path that makes much of God and others. It's the path that values humility and humanity simultaneously. As we follow Christ, we needn't be overly concerned or overly nonchalant about our social media presence. Instead, we need to embrace self-forgetfulness as a virtue.

Everything about social media is better when we think of ourselves less. C. S. Lewis said that "humility is not thinking less of yourself, but thinking of yourself less."[2]

This kind of self-forgetful living is truly an art and is not easy to grow in. In my experience, the direct pursuit of humility is difficult. When you pursue humility as a virtue, you begin censoring your conversations. You try to speak less of yourself and more of others. You don't want others to praise you, but you seek to heap praise on others. The more you work at it, the better you get at deflecting applause and belittling your accomplishments. Soon you feel confident that you're a humble person.

But humble people don't feel confident in their humility. In fact, humble people aren't really marked by deflecting credit or putting themselves down. Lewis gives us insight into what an interaction with a self-forgetful (humble) person might look like:

To even get near [humility], even for a moment, is like a drink of cold water to a man in a desert. Do not imagine that if you meet a really humble man he will be what most people call "humble" nowadays: he will not be a sort of greasy, smarmy person, who is always telling you that, of course, he is nobody. Probably all you will think about him is that he seemed a cheerful, intelligent chap who took a real interest in what you said to him. If you do dislike him, it will be because you feel a little envious of anyone who seems to enjoy life so easily. He will not be thinking about humility: he will not be thinking about himself at all.[3]

There's only one way to truly grow in self-forgetfulness, and it isn't by trying hard to be humble. It's by worshiping and pursuing God.

We learn to forget about ourselves when we are truly and sincerely wowed by someone or something else.

> Everything about social media
> is better when we think of
> ourselves less.

When I saw my wife walking down the aisle on our wedding day, it was a totally self-forgetful moment. I was enthralled with her beauty. She was the most stunningly gorgeous woman in the world to me, and all of my attention was fixed on her. I could have been standing there in cargo jeans and a cut-off shirt and not cared a bit. That's what it looks like to forget self.

When the white-hot flame of the gospel whips against the icy chambers of our heart, we are melted by the love of God. In an instant, God has become glorious to us. The perfect redemptive plan of God has been set before us, and we see our place in it all. We are filled with joy. God is real and He loves us! In that moment, we have forgotten about ourselves.

But the self doesn't take well to being forgotten. Soon we have forgotten the feeling of being raptured by the grace of God, and we are back to being overly self-conscious. We are no longer in awe of Him, and we need to be wowed all over again.

I contend that the only way for us to engage in social media in a healthy way is for us to be regularly wowed by the gospel. Otherwise, we'll drift right back into habitual self-absorption and self-exaltation through the medium of social media.

Limiting selfies to one per week isn't going to do it. Trying our best to comment more on the status updates of others rather than our own isn't the answer. Censoring our every conversation to make sure it doesn't reek of narcissism isn't enough. We can run ourselves ragged trying to find a grid through which to filter our narcissistic online tendencies, and we will still end up just as self-indulgent as when we started.

Instead, we need to be overwhelmed all over again with the sacrificial, self-denying, humility-displaying cross of Jesus Christ. And we need this to happen every day. Only by kneeling at the foot of the cross and taking up our own cross daily can we find a true antidote to the narcissism that threatens our soul.

Reflection Questions

Do you often feel the tug to check on your status updates for likes, comments, and overall approval? What are the feelings you experience when you check?

What are things that stir your affection for Christ and remind you of the wonder of the gospel?

How can you develop habits and rhythms in your life that encourage an ongoing love and appreciation for the gospel? How about in your family's life?

PEOPLE:
THE SACRIFICES WE MAKE

"There is nothing on this earth more to be prized than true friendship."

—Thomas Aquinas

I once had the opportunity to visit an orphanage for children with disabilities in a town on the border of Texas and Mexico called Piedras Negras. This area was relatively small and very poor. The youth group I led partnered with a ministry there to serve some of the locals, help with some construction projects, and lead VBS Bible studies for the children.

Midweek, we made a trip to a nearby orphanage that served children with special needs. The facility was not in great condition, and the staffers were clearly overwhelmed. They welcomed us kindly and allowed us to talk to and pray with the children, but they weren't able to offer much supervision or guidance. We were kind of on our own.

As I ambled cautiously from room to room, I watched as the students began to engage with the children, making them laugh. It was evident our presence was appreciated.

Many of the children could not speak, and some required wheelchairs or constant assistance day and night. Our students didn't miss a beat. They jumped right in and loved these children as if they knew them, as if they were friends and family.

I continued to walk the halls and survey the rest of the grounds. My heart was grieved not only by the condition of the children, but by the lack of resources they had there. I began to whisper prayers to God, admitting it was hard to understand this kind of suffering.

As I was praying, I happened upon a room with an older boy who was lying on his back in his bed, staring at the ceiling, and making noises as if he wanted help. I later learned that he had been diagnosed with severe cerebral palsy. I looked around to see if there were anyone else around. I felt very ill-equipped to meet any needs, and I was concerned I was about to get in way over my head. By God's providence, I was the only one around.

> This poor child was stuck in a white-walled room, bedridden, without parents, and without others to love and care for him in that moment. Nothing about this situation was OK.

I tiptoed into the room, the stale air of the facility palpable to me now.

"Everything OK in here?" I asked in a sheepish voice.

I felt like an idiot. Of course things weren't OK. This poor child was stuck in a white-walled room, bedridden, without

128

parents, and without others to love and care for him in that moment. Nothing about this situation was OK.

The boy reached his hands forward and made the noises again. I had to do something. So I did the only thing I knew to do. I reached out my hand and grabbed his. Instantly, he gripped my hand tightly. I was surprised by his strength. There was an urgency to it. He pulled me closer to his bedside, and I looked down to begin talking with him.

To this day, I do not remember his name. If there were a hundred faces in a lineup, I don't think I could pick him out except for one major distinction.

His eyes.

When he grasped my hand that day and I peered down into his face, our eyes connected in a way so special that I still can't fully articulate the experience. It was as though my soul had been simultaneously gripped along with my hand. A truth so essential and so fundamental had been revealed to me, and I was ashamed and embarrassed that I hadn't known it sooner. Or maybe I did, but I had lived as though I didn't believe it.

This young boy was a person, and he mattered to me.

He didn't speak to me because he wasn't able to. We didn't discuss theology; I didn't learn what his favorite color is; and we may never see each other again. But in that moment, with his hand clenching mine and his eyes peering into mine, I knew I was changed. My eyes welled with tears as we looked at one another. Psychologically it doesn't make any sense, but I'm convinced that in that moment we understood each other. I knew he wanted things to be different, and he knew that I felt helpless to offer much of anything.

He and I sat there together for the rest of the day. Sometimes I talked to him. Other times I prayed with him, for him, and over him. But most of the time we just sat. We just existed in the same room for a little while—two people who appreciated the fact that the other was there. There was a holiness to those moments.

Until that experience, I often felt that I needed to offer people my words. Whether it be words of encouragement, words of truth, words of affirmation, or words of rebuke, I felt this tug to say something profound that would miraculously make everything OK.

> People aren't projects or commodities. They aren't profile pictures and Instagram feeds. People's lives aren't defined by a mashup of their top 20 Facebook posts. Each human being is an image bearer of God.

That day this young boy taught me something new. Sometimes the ministry of presence is the most powerful ministry we can offer to others. Being there, embracing another human being in their suffering, acknowledging them as a person, and loving them through the silence is what is sometimes needed most.

People need to be reminded that they are valuable, that they have worth and dignity by virtue of simply being a human being. People aren't projects or commodities. They aren't profile pictures and Instagram feeds. People's lives aren't defined by a mashup of their top 20 Facebook posts. Each human being is an image bearer of God.

I was able to apply my theological framework to my

experience later. This young boy mattered to me because he matters to God. I didn't know he existed before that day, but it didn't matter. The connection we felt was a connection because we are all uniquely created to reflect God. I was learning about the Trinity in a Mexican orphanage, and I had no idea at the time.

Wired for Connectivity

There are few if any Christian doctrines as mind-boggling and essential as the doctrine of the Trinity. The one God of the Bible is also three distinct persons simultaneously, while retaining singularity in essence and equality in distinction. All human analogies attempting to fully explain this reality break down. Despite being difficult to comprehend, the concept of the Trinity is taught throughout the Scriptures in various places.

The Trinity is one of the many things that makes Christianity unique among world religions. Some monotheists label Christians as pagans because monotheists wrongly assume that Christians believe in three gods. Pluralists, on the other hand, cannot embrace Christianity because of the Christian claim that our God is one. We are a difficult group to categorize.

The uniqueness of the Trinity is revealed in the first book of the Bible. After God creates the world, light, darkness, sun, moon, stars, vegetation, oceans, and animals, He then turns His attention to human beings. He will create mankind. Unlike the rest of creation, God pauses for a moment of dialogue before creating mankind:

"Let **us** make man in **our** image after our likeness" (Gen. 1:26).

Here, some wrongly assume that God must be discussing His creation with the angels or some other unknown audience. However, the Bible is clear from this moment on that human beings were explicitly created in the image of God, and not angels. At no place in the Scriptures are angels mentioned as being co-creators with God. Therefore, in light of Genesis 1 we must conclude that there's a plurality to the godhead. God takes counsel within Himself to create mankind.

This is important.

We were made to carry some of God's attributes and mirror His likeness. We are not God, but we are made in the image of God. Like the moon has no light of its own and can only reflect the light of the sun, we too were created to reflect the glory of the greater light.

But the beauty, majesty, and complexity of God dwarfs the sun, despite the sun's own significant uniqueness and glory. To be a reflection of God is the highest of all honors, the greatest call one could ever hope to have. To learn what God is like is to understand what we were meant to reflect. The more we know about God, the more we understand about God's original intent for us.

And so the plurality of the Godhead gives us insight as to why we have a need for others. God exists eternally in relationship—Father, Son, and Spirit. God is relational. Therefore, as image bearers, we are incomplete without relationships.

Community, friendship, and relational connectivity are integral and essential to what it means to be human. We are wired for it.

When I grabbed the hand of that older boy, I was tapping into something that is innate within the human soul. In my heart, I was recognizing not only another human being's God-given value, but also our hardwiring for relationship.

Good Intentions

My goal when I signed up for social media my freshman year of college was to connect with old friends and maybe make some new ones. It seemed like a helpful tool that might give me a chance to meet people whom I might not normally get to meet in my everyday walking around campus. And since social media's primary draw is connectivity, it's no wonder that many people sign up for the same reasons I did. It's meant to facilitate and foster relationships.

> Community, friendship, and relational connectivity are integral and essential to what it means to be human. We are wired for it.

The irony is that we often neglect our primary relationships in pursuit of online connectivity, which was supposed to be a tool for relationships, not a replacement of real-life ones.

Somewhere along the way, our idealistic aims for social media tend to get lost. What began as a hope to connect with others turns into something else entirely, and we're often left wondering what happened.

My wife and I plug our phones in at night near our nightstands. Before my time away from social media, there were numerous nights that our faces were aglow with the light of our phones as we mindlessly scrolled through the daily digest of new posts. That seems relatively harmless, and in some cases perhaps it is; but it didn't stop there for us, and it doesn't stop there for many others.

Once I started looking for it, I noticed that people were immersed in their phones everywhere I went. A couple sitting at a restaurant on a date were both scrolling through Instagram. Eight out of the ten people standing with me on the escalator were checking Facebook. As I walked out of the mall, I realized that at least half of the people there were largely unaware of others around them because they were looking at their phones most of the time.

> It's ironic how unsocial we can be while using social media.

It's ironic how unsocial we can be while using social media.

Faux Friendships

Let me be clear: social media serves as good scaffolding for relationships. Using technology to meet new people or create new friendships through current friendships is fine. But as the statistics show, social media is a poor substitute for the foundational relationships in your life.

We all know that our Facebook friends list can be inflated. If you don't think that's true, count the number of friends that come to your next birthday party. If it isn't 1,784, then you probably have an inflated friends list.

Take heart; I don't think the answer to this issue is to publicly purge your friends list by posting an announcement online, saying, "I will be cutting my friends list in half today. This has been getting out of hand, and I hope you make the cut."

Don't laugh (or cringe). I have seen these kinds of posts multiple times.

We should be aware of "friend" inflation, though, to ensure that we're not buying into a false narrative about our friendships. Because we are so committed to scrolling and keeping up-to-date with everyone, we can sometimes fool ourselves into believing that just because we know what is happening in the lives of others, we are staying connected to them. That's a false assumption. I'm updated every day by phone alerts about the status of the Houston Texans football team, but I have no relationship at all with them. I watch them play on my television set.

> Just because you are updated on someone's life informationally, doesn't mean you are connected with them relationally.

Many of us have about the same level of relational capital with some we would consider to be our "good friends" as I do with the Texans. Being updated on someone's life informationally doesn't mean you are connected with them relationally. We are *faux* friends with more people than we would care to admit.

This isn't true just for the online junkies either. The tendency at this point would be to think, "Not me; I got tons of friends!" Ask yourself, though, do you tend to take for granted that you're in good standing with your friends because you know when they last checked into the gym? When's the last time you had a chance to ask a friend how things are going and give them a real hug in person, not a virtual one?

If the statistics are true (and they are), the main issue with faux friends is that we are often only keeping up with the highlight reels of our friends' lives and usually not the intricate details of what is actually going on with them.

Status Update	Faux Friend Lie	Reality
Update from Susie with the little one at home: "Reading Chronicles of Narnia! He's already a genius." #cslewis #aslan *Filtered Instagram Post*	Thoughts: It's great to see that Susie is educating and connecting with her kid. She is such a great mom.	You haven't spoken to Susie in three weeks. You surmise that she's killing it as a mom, yet you don't know that she has been struggling with feelings of inadequacy.
Update from John, who is on a mountaintop: "Loving a relaxing vacation away. What a view!"	Thoughts: Man, John must be doing great at work to take that kind of vacation.	It's been a couple of months since you two have spoken in person. He actually just lost his job, and he's getting away to recoup.
Update from the Smiths, long-time friends: "Celebrating 12 years of marriage. Roses, wine, and good food."	Thoughts: That's great. I'm so happy to see that they are thriving after 12 years of marriage.	Though you hung out with this couple a few months ago, you don't know that their marriage has been in a deep rut, and this anniversary dinner is an attempt to pull them out of it.

It's very hard to "break bread with one another" simply by observing your friend's dining habits online. That kind of friendship *on our own terms* is nonexistent in the Scriptures, and not just because of advances in technology. We were never meant to *only* have relationships that we can view at a distance.

Don't get me wrong, the highlight reel isn't all bad either. In fact, sometimes it really is a joy to see.

- First kiss at the wedding
- Baby showers
- Birthday get-togethers each year
- Your teenager's first car driver's license.
- Mom's first time holding her baby
- First-time home buyers
- Adoption updates (personal favorite)
- The bittersweet day they leave for college
- Honeymoon on the beach
- Funny family vine videos
- Church gatherings and groups
- The look on your face when you pay for college
- Anniversary dinner
- Holidays with the family
- First day of school with smiling children
- The coffee on the porch with the one you love
- Graduation parties
- Football games with friends
- Last day of school with terrified parents
- The encouraging words to others on their journey

Man, the highlight reel can be awesome. In fact, I want to emphasize how much I actually enjoy it!

We simply need to be careful not to rely solely on the highlight reel to support our relationships all of the time. Sometimes we're reminded of that when friends actually share some of their lowlights. Things like loss of employment, death of a loved one, miscarriages, sickness, fatigue, anxiety, depression, and so much more.

Despite the new "reaction" feature on Facebook, online reactions and engagements are often not enough. It can be an initial way to show concern and compassion, but we must reject the temptation to just consume this information without sometimes getting more involved personally. The amount of good that social media has done to remind people that they are not alone in their suffering is unfathomable. It should be noted and praised. But there's a reason that the expression *feeling alone in a crowded room* exists, and, sadly, social media can contribute to that feeling.

If possible and appropriate, we should reach out to others in ways that go beyond social media. We can extend the grace and love of Christ by stepping into others' hardships with gentleness and care. By being personable and not always keeping others at arm's-length (or assuming that's what they desire), we can be a tangible expression of God's love to others.

The Iron Worker

The Scriptures give us insight into the nature of relationship as designed by God. Not only were we created for relationships as image bearers, but these relationships were meant to shape us and mold us. Proverbs uses the analogy,

"As iron sharpens iron, so one man sharpens another" (Prov. 27:17).

This text has been quoted widely as a way to promote togetherness and community. We are meant to sharpen one another and to spur one another to love and good works (Heb. 10:24). But if you consider the nature of ironwork, there is a nastier and more primal side to this analogy. A cursory study will give you three ingredients to the work of sharpening iron:

Fire—The metal is heated in a furnace to create malleableness.

Force—The metal is struck with a hammer or object to form and sharpen the edges.

Friction—The metal is put under repeated pressure at certain angles. The combination of fire and force refine the edge.

This entire process is repeated over and over, requiring time and consistency. The analogy of Scripture then is that healthy relationships have a love (fire) to them that creates vulnerability (malleableness). This vulnerability is never abused to destroy us (the metal) but to shape us and form us. It requires difficulty (force) and even stress (friction) at times. Certain seasons (angles) of our relationships may not be pleasant and could even be inconvenient, but the end result is worth it.

Social media doesn't provide all of the necessary tools that true *ironwork* requires.

Often social media relationships are built around convenience, and therefore it is much easier for us to slip out of the vice to avoid the friction, fire, and force that are coming.

We can simply log off when things get uncomfortable. Again, it is much more difficult to walk out on someone in person than it is to turn your phone off.

> Social media does not provide all of the necessary tools that true ironwork requires.

Face-to-face relationships require the fruit of the Spirit—love, joy, peace, patience, kindness, goodness, faithfulness, gentleness, and self-control (Gal. 5:22–23)—in a more hands-on way. They guarantee for us that we will have people that stay over too late, talk too much, care too little, stand too close, chew too loudly, laugh too weirdly, and sing too badly. These relationships become the laboratory for sanctification. These realities of relationships are necessary for the iron workshop that God has designed to make us more like Jesus.

Of course, these aren't the only things we experience in up-close relationships.

These face-to-face interactions also guarantee that you might laugh until you cry or cry until you laugh. You might have a conversation that lasts until midnight because it's just that good. It's the bonfires, the dancing, the karaoke, the board games, the movie nights, the Bible studies, the picnics, the dinners that make you loosen your belt a notch, and so much more that can't be replicated online.

These are the features of real-life community that offers us a glimpse of eternity. It's not a coincidence that one of our first appointments in the New Jerusalem will be a marriage supper celebration. There, we will experience gospel community like we never have before. Real-life community offers moments today that are glimpses of what's to come.

And the most mysterious truth about the ironworker's shop is the ironworker Himself. Jesus is faithfully shaping and molding us into His image there.

The gospel tells us that even though we are made in the image of God and wired for relationship, we are broken and frayed by sin. Before Christ, we are far from how God designed us. But then God makes us alive together with Christ through our faith in His death and resurrection, and He continues to restore the things that are broken in us.

> Real-life community offers moments today that are glimpses of what's to come.

Now in Christ, we are being remade into the image of God again. Jesus, the great ironworker, is using fire, force, and friction in our lives to shape us daily. And He is doing it through other people. Our real, tangible relationships are being used to chip away at our selfish tendencies, sharpen our love and passion, and blunt our anger and entitlement. That's the reason I saw something holy in that older boy's eyes in Mexico. Real-life human interaction is serious business because it comes from God. C. S. Lewis helps articulate what I was feeling:

There are no ordinary people. You have never talked to a mere mortal. Nations, cultures, arts, civilizations— these are mortal, and their life is to ours as the life of a gnat. But it is immortals whom we joke with, work with, marry, snub and exploit—immortal horrors or everlasting splendors. This does not mean that we are to be perpetually solemn. We must play. But our merriment must be of that kind (and it is, in fact, the merriest kind) which exists between people who have, from the outset, taken each other seriously—no flippancy, no superiority, no presumption.[1]

That day in Mexico I felt the seriousness Lewis is talking about. We must approach social media with this same mindset. Does that mean we should be overly-serious killjoys? Of course not! As Lewis said, "We must play"! But our joy must be grounded in a kind of seriousness that reminds us we cannot take one another for granted. Social media is fantastic scaffolding for relationships, but it doesn't have what it takes to hold the full weight of God's design for community. If we use it to supplement relationships and bring color and life to those around us, it can be the greatest ally. If it detracts from our real-life relationships, alienating us from those we claim to hold dearest, we must change how we use it.

> Social media is fantastic scaffolding for relationships, but it doesn't have what it takes to hold the full weight of God's design for community.

Sacrifice

Every day we are forced to make sacrifices. What will we choose to cut out of our day in order to fit in the things that matter most? My plea is that we don't allow people to be cut out of our lives unwittingly because we're drowning in the digital sea. We can think we're just out for a leisurely swim, but then drift away from the people we're meant to be with the most.

The model that Jesus set for us was one of great care and love toward others. He was always present in the moment, as we see in the following stories.

Walking through a crowd of people, Jesus stopped because a woman with a debilitating disease had touched His garment. He slowed down to heal her (Luke 8:40–48).

After a tiring journey, Jesus stopped at a well in order to cross paths with a Samaritan woman having relationship issues. He offered her a whole new life (John 4:1–42).

Crowds pressing around Him, Jesus paused to point to someone up in a tree. A dishonest tax-collector had climbed up to get a better look. Jesus had dinner with the man and forgave him of all his many sins (Luke 19:1–10).

In the same town, crowds followed Jesus around; as He was leaving, a blind man cried out, "Jesus, Son of David have mercy on me!" (Mark 10:47). Some in the crowd rebuked him, but Jesus stopped to heal the man.

Jesus, tired from the day's labor, was brought little children to pray over. The disciples rebuked the people and tried to shoo the children away. Jesus stopped them and said, "Let the little children come to me and do not hinder them" (Matt. 19:14).

Jesus didn't sacrifice His ministry to people, no matter the pressures that were upon Him. He came to "give his life as a ransom for many" (Matt. 20:28). He was not only *unwilling* to allow others to be forsaken and forgotten, but He was also *willing* to be forsaken and forgotten for them. He bore the cross not only to reconnect us to God, but also to reconnect us to one another. It's because of Christ's sacrifice for the world that we are being increasingly remade into God's image, as lovers of Him and other people too.

Let's determine to use social media as a tool to love others the way Christ has loved us, and not at the expense of our real-life relationships.

Reflection Questions

👆 Who are the people in your life that you know God has called you to spend meaningful time with?

👆 How can you utilize social media to help supplement and cultivate these relationships?

👆 How can you show Christlike love for others online and offline?

GLORY:
THE THING WE ALL CRAVE

"Define yourself radically as one beloved by God. This is the true self. Every other identity is illusion."

—Brennan Manning

With 50 meters to go in the 200-meter men's butterfly final in the Rio Olympics, it was no surprise to see Michael Phelps leading the pack with World Champion Chad Le Clos close behind. The two storied rivals had exchanged words leading up to the events, and now the moment of truth had arrived.

As they neared the finish, Michael Phelps dug deep and, as all Americans had seen him do 19 times before, finished strong to the win the gold medal.

The crowd went crazy. The roar in the Aquatics Center was thunderous as fans lavished their praise on Phelps, one of the greatest Olympians of all time who continued to show his dominance in the sport.

Then Phelps did something that created some controversy on social media. As he straddled the lane buoys to look over at the final time, he stretched out his arms and gave the double "bring it on" hand motion from Neo in The Matrix. In other words, he was calling for more applause. This did not sit well with some:

> Y'all know we'd all hate Michael Phelps' attitude if he was from any other country. . . . Who the h*ll does a summoning motion for applause?

> Unpopular opinion: Michael Phelps is way too arrogant and drives me crazy.

> Katie Ladecky hugged her competitors when she won, and Michael Phelps is asking for applause.[1]

To be clear, this was not the prevailing sentiment surrounding Phelps gestures, and no one has enjoyed his dominance over the years more than I have. (I'm kind of a "homer" in that way.) The interesting point here is that as a society we have no problem lavishing praise on our celebrities and/or our athletes, but we take issue with their asking for it. The prevailing thought seems to be, "We'll give you all the accolades we want; just pretend like you don't really want to receive them."

Phelps was simply calling for what most of us were eager to give him—glory.

Inconsolable Secret

One of the greatest thinkers of the twentieth century was C. S. Lewis. Many in our culture recognize him as the author of The Chronicles of Narnia, but Lewis's works are vast and various. They span from science fiction novels to wise counsel on grieving to the basic tenets of Christianity.

In a short essay entitled, "The Weight of Glory," Lewis pinpoints the inescapable longing that exists in the human heart for glory. This longing is why athletes like Phelps will spend thousands of hours training, dieting, and even doing suction cup therapy on their muscles in the hope of receiving 90 seconds of applause in the arena. Lewis calls this quest for glory the "inconsolable secret" inside every person. The secret is that there is a longing in us that this world cannot satisfy, and therefore we conclude that we have been created for another world—an eternal one.

We all have this longing for more, and there are times in our lives when the tug is especially strong. We define our incompleteness the best we can. Some call it nostalgia, the feeling that sweeps across us when we recall a good time. Others call it romanticism or post-adolescent angst. Some believe that it's primarily exposure to beauty that causes these feelings. But Lewis believes that these are all pale substitutes for the real thing:

> These things—the beauty, the memory of our own past—are good images of what we really desire; but if they are mistaken for the thing itself they turn into dumb idols, breaking the hearts of their worshippers. For they are not the thing itself; they are only the scent of a flower we have not found, the echo of a tune we have not heard, news from a country we have never yet visited. Do you think I am trying to weave a spell? Perhaps I am; but remember your fairy tales. Spells are used for breaking enchantments as well as for inducing them. And you and I have need of the strongest spell that can be found to wake us from the evil enchantment

of worldliness which has been laid upon us for nearly a hundred years. Almost our whole education has been directed to silencing this shy, persistent, inner voice; almost all our modern philosophies have been devised to convince us that the good of man is to be found on this earth.[2]

There is no consolation on earth for our inconsolable, eternal souls, but that doesn't stop us from searching for it with all our might.

Phelps's motion for more applause is a reflection of what goes on inside each of our hearts every day. We work diligently to find something to medicate this longing in us, and nothing quite scratches the itch like glory can.

> There is no consolation on earth for our inconsolable, eternal souls, but that doesn't stop us from searching for it with all our might.

Glory is the high regard and honor we all desire; it is the approval, acceptance, and delight we seek from others. The interesting thing is, we are not only all wired to long for glory, but we are also wired to give glory to others. In others words, glory can be a noun and a verb.

We long for glory (delight) from others, and we glory (delight) in others. In both cases, the glory is usually attached to some kind of accomplishment.

The Laboratory of Glory

Social media is the perfect place for glory.

Let's face it, most of us will not be Michael Phelps. I'm not knocking the dreamer who hopes to have that kind of success, picking up where Phelps left off. But for most of us, Olympic glory is not in our future. There will be a mundaneness to much of our lives, and I want to suggest that that's perfectly OK.

Yet social media is an arena where the relatively unknown can find some applause. Likes, favorites, retweets, comments, and shares are like virtual cheering sections for us. If you don't think I'm right about this, consider the last time you posted a picture, video, or update. Did you go back soon after to see what the response was?

Picture yourself, like Michael Phelps, calling for the applause of the digital audience. It changes things a little, doesn't it?

> Social media is an arena where the relatively unknown can find some applause.

On the flip side, social media also gives us the opportunity to glory in others. That's why celebrities and athletes boast millions of followers on their profiles. These celebrities provide a service of sorts. They provide a selfie (sometimes scantily clad), and we provide the cheering section.

The online glory culture creates some sticky situations sometimes.

One is that it's possible to become digitally bitter toward

someone whom you actually like in person. If they are too outspoken for your tastes, and their posts begin to seem like a call for applause, you might start to develop some mild irritation in your heart. This tension will likely cross over from online to offline no matter how hard you fight against it. (For many people, this is especially true when it comes to political commentary.)

It can be tough to figure out where to draw the line, too. If we all contain the inconsolable secret (the unquenchable desire for glory), then we are all susceptible to this desire spinning out of control. So how do we combat our glory hunger? How do we decide if it's true that Katie Ledecky is sufficiently humble, but Michael Phelps is unreasonably proud?

The Consolation of Christ

Since childhood, I've always been an extremely competitive person. I was the youngest of three children, and I expected to win at everything I did no matter the age gap. My brother was 2 feet taller than me, yet that didn't stop me from fighting and clawing to win every argument and game, or storm from the house in tears when I lost. After coming to Christ, I realized the root of this struggle and began learning how to submit my unhealthy competitiveness to Christ.

As an angry, competitive kid, though, there was nothing more humiliating to me than receiving the consolation prize. In single elimination tournament play, one loss not only knocks you out of championship contention, but it places your team on the other side of the bracket where you play for the consolation trophy.

> The Lord has a way of using the despised things of the world to be his source of delight.

Everything about the word *consolation* grinds against my unnaturally competitive heart. The last thing I want is to be consoled after a loss. Any kind of consolations means I was inadequate. I wasn't quite enough. I didn't quite make the cut. I wasn't up to snuff.

I failed.

The thing I've been learning, though, is that the Lord has a way of using the despised things of the world to be His source of delight.

In a confrontation with the religious elite of His day, Jesus had some interesting things to say about the nature of man's heart and our longing for glory:

I do not receive glory from people. But I know that you do not have the love of God within you. I have come in my Father's name, and you do not receive me. If another comes in his own name, you will receive him. How can you believe, when you receive glory from one another and do not seek the glory that comes from the only God? (John 5:41–44).

Jesus drew a stark contrast between Himself and the Pharisees. Notice he didn't point out their religious practices as a point of contention. He goes deeper. He said they receive glory from one another but wouldn't receive a Man who came to give and receive glory to Another. Jesus did everything for the glory of His Father. He was secure in His identity and sought to bring glory to God alone. That was His particular glory. The Pharisees couldn't receive Jesus because they were looking for someone who wanted to receive glory for himself just as they did. They wanted someone who would play their game by their rules. Jesus was not that guy.

Jesus does give them insight, though, into what the inconsolable soul needs and desires more than anything else—"the glory that comes from the only God."

This calls for some consideration. Surely it's blasphemous to assert that we should seek glory from God, right? After all, the Bible says elsewhere that God will not share His glory with another (Isa. 42:8).

Here Jesus is referring to our deep longing for approval, acceptance, and delight. This "glory" is what drives us to incessantly post more and more updates of our lives, more and more selfies at just the right angle, and more and more gym check-ins for others to admire (or disdain). Attention-grabbing may be fleeting, but it's like cold water to the burn of our glory-hungry souls. It doesn't fix the problem permanently, but it sure eases the pain for a little while.

We can fall into the same trap as the Pharisees settling for temporary fixes of glory online, rather than seeking after the eternal glory offered to us in Jesus. To a struggling church in Corinth, Paul wrote,

> For this light momentary affliction is preparing for us an eternal weight of glory beyond comparison (2 Cor. 4:17).

> Attention is fleeting, but it is like cold water to the burn of our glory-hungry souls. It doesn't fix the problem permanently, but it sure eases the pain for a little while.

This promise of glory is no small thing. It's the fulfillment of the soul's deepest desire—the approval, delight, and acceptance of God Himself.

I often imagine standing before the throne of God one day. Humbled, I'm there to receive His opinion of me; His judgment of who I am and what I've done. When I consider it, there's a level of anxiety that comes over me. What will He say? How will I fare?

The Christian doesn't have to contemplate or anxiously consider God's response. He has already given it to us in Christ. "Well done, good and faithful servant" (Matt. 25:21) will apply to us too.

For the Christian, all that we are and everything that we have done (or failed to do) will not be held up to scrutiny in that moment. Instead, it will be the spotless record of Jesus Christ that will lie open before the Judge's face. The aroma of a perfect and blameless life will fill the courtroom, and we will not only be acquitted of all our guilt, but will be praised for all of Christ's accomplishments. This is what Martin Luther called "the great exchange."

We not only are forgiven because Jesus paid our debts, but we are eternally approved, delighted in, and accepted because Jesus imputed His righteousness to us.

We will receive glory.

C. S. Lewis unpacks it more poetically than I can:

The promise of glory is the promise, almost incredible and only possible by the work of Christ, that some of us, that any of us who really chooses, shall actually survive that [final] examination, shall find approval, shall please God. To please God . . . to be a real ingredient in the divine happiness . . . to be loved by God, not merely pitied, but delighted in as an artist delights in his work or a father in a son—it seems impossible, a weight or burden of glory which our thoughts can hardly sustain. But so it is.[3]

We not only get to be a part of the divine happiness, but a real ingredient in it.

> We not only get to be a part of the divine happiness, but a real ingredient in it.

Only God can take the worldly meaning of consolation and flip it on its head. No one wants to have to settle for the consolation prize. But in Christ, we receive our soul's consolation; and it truly is the greatest prize of all. All other glories are weak substitutes compared to the future glory we will receive—a glory we receive tastes of even now. To seek the glory that comes from God is our highest calling and our greatest good.

Balance vs. Security

The clear challenge before us now is to make sure we're not seeking glory and approval from others while we engage on social media platforms. In light of what we've discussed, won't everything we do now just seem like a glory grab?

Conventional wisdom would tell us to try to find a balance. We don't want to be too self-conscious or utterly oblivious. We need to find a happy medium that doesn't give the impression that we're trying too hard to show restraint, but isn't overly self-exalting either. And, of course, there's always the danger of letting our religious zeal online turn into the pursuit of vainglory like what happened with the Pharisees. That's some of the thinking, anyway. So, we often try to strike a balance.

However, a balance is not the answer to our glory hunger. We can't solve our sin problem by simply trying to manage it. We must overcome our sin problem with a hearty belief in gospel truth and a robust return to gospel clarity.

> We must reply to our sin problem with a hearty belief in gospel truth and a robust return to gospel clarity.

As we engage in social media, we need to simply be reminded of our position in Christ. Our approval is already more secure than a loaded Brink's truck. God's delighted disposition toward us is as unchanging as the sun's daily appointment of rising and setting.

You are deeply, unchangeably loved by God. This is who you are. Nothing else is more life-changing, soul-stirring, and behavior-modifying than that.

If this is our foundational springboard into the realm of social media, we won't have to be overly concerned about what we should or shouldn't post, what we should or shouldn't like, and what we should or shouldn't comment on.

The gospel becomes our guide.

As we abide in Christ and grow in wisdom and maturity, we won't need online laws to follow so much as direction from the Spirit.

Let me say this: a Christian's social media page does not have to be only Scripture. I'm going to venture out and say it probably shouldn't be only Scripture. We are not merely "Scripture-bots," churning out only Bible verses and deep quotes from our favorite theologians. We are people who have been redeemed by a loving, caring, and creative God, and our social media pages should reflect that truth.

Reflection Questions

When you survey your posts, where do you find signs of glory hunger?

What are the faulty beliefs driving those posts? What gospel truths are you struggling to believe?

When you think about God's disposition toward you, what comes to mind? If it's not delight, how do you think God feels about you? Why?

How does the truth of the gospel inform and reshape your image of God and the resultant emotions attached to that?

HEART:
THE UNGUARDED WELL

"Blessed are the pure in heart, for they shall see God."
—Jesus

In many instances, wells have spiritual significance in the Bible. Isaac met his wife Rebekah at a well. Jacob dug a series of wells on the land that would one day be Israel. And Jesus met a woman at one of Jacob's wells and offered her living water.

A well represents life. Everyone needs water to live, and a well is the place to get it. Many times, wells were placed at the center of town in order to provide a common, centralized location for everyone to get the family water supply for the day. A well served as the site of a necessary resource a town needed to survive. If there was no water, there could be no town.

In Scripture, the heart is the source of the human being. It's almost never referred to as the four-chambered organ that keeps blood circulating in the body. The heart is the seat of our will and affections. It's from the heart that we speak, act, love, hate, grieve, rejoice, give, withhold, lust, and worship. When the Bible speaks about guarding your heart, it's talking about guarding the center of your spiritual life, the very essence of who you are. When God grieves over our sin, He attributes it to our hearts. When Jesus rebuked the Pharisees, he did so because, despite their religious words, their hearts were far from Him. It's fair to say that God is deeply concerned with the condition of our hearts.

If you took a survey of twenty friends and asked them their opinions about social media, most of them would acknowledge that there are at least some drawbacks that go with it. Whether it's excessive time-wasting or information overload, most everyone recognizes that the constant connectivity of social media creates some issues in us.

Some of us fall into the ditch of comparison (SCS) and struggle to get back out. We can be drawn into online quarrels. Others of us find lust and pornography a fierce battle we cannot seem to overcome. Sexting and/or online encounters are statistically common. Some find themselves scrolling the pages of old flames or, even more tragically, fall into infidelity after reconnecting with them.

The list of pitfalls, some small and others gigantic, are legion. And we all know it, though sometimes we choose to ignore it.

Throughout this project, I have frequently found myself in a conversation with someone who says something like, "I think I'm just going to quit this whole social media thing altogether." This usually comes after a lament about social media's negative aspects or because of an inability to get a handle on an issue that social media seems to cause.

SOCIAL MEDIA PITFALLS

- Wasting Time
- Unhealthy Comparison
- Digital Infidelity
- Lust/Pornography
- Anger/Quarreling
- Bitterness/Strife
- Search for Approval
- Narcissistic Tendencies
- Obsessive Habits/ Addiction
- Fear of Missing Out (FOMO)
- Lack of Real Friendships

Without a doubt, social media can exacerbate sin and folly.

But I contend that social media is not at the root of these issues. It's easy to lay the blame for some of our woes at the feet of social media, but Facebook is not the cause of infidelity. Instagram is not the cause of unhealthy comparison. Twitter is not the root of our anger. Snapchat is not the culprit behind our lust. We struggle with all of these things because of the condition of our hearts.

We have left the well unguarded, and we are looking for someone or something to blame.

Heart Disease

Jeremiah laments the condition of the human heart as he surveys the brokenness of the nation of Israel:

The heart is deceitful above all things, and desperately sick; who can understand it? (Jer. 2:12–13).

Israel constantly battled idolatry and unbelief despite God's constant displays of power and grace in their midst. Not only had God endured their sin and displayed His faithfulness by redeeming them repeatedly, He had also given them constant warnings that if they did not address their wicked, unbelieving hearts, they would face judgment and correction. Jeremiah wrote this lament during a time when Israel was experiencing the consequences of her sin—exile and ruin.

The negative patterns we find ourselves caught in on social media have little to do with the medium itself. Social media is morally neutral, but it can magnify the brokenness and idolatry of our hearts. It can reveal just how dissatisfied we are with God and how we often forsake the things of God in our search for joy, peace, and pleasure. Social media doesn't create heart sickness; it just reveals it.

In the 1800s, tens of thousands of people were dying of cholera in London. With 2.5 million people crammed into a small metropolitan area, the concerns were beginning to heighten. Many of the physicians of that day believed the disease spread through airborne means. When people caught wind of a foul stench in the air, they would cover their mouths and flee for safety. The city was in disarray.

A man named John Snow had another theory. His suspicions were formed around the observation that there was a lack of sanitation; there just wasn't a proper sewage system in place. He figured that if the bacteria created by a lack of city services could somehow creep into the city populace, an outbreak could ensue such as they were experiencing. But he needed evidence to prove his theory.

Snow began tracking the deaths on a paper map of London. His thinking was that if he could find a correlation between location and the cases of sickness, he would be able to further prove his theory. At first, the locations seemed scattered. The cases of cholera were not all in one place near an unsanitary landfill or human waste dump. Then he found what he was looking for.

Every single case of cholera was connected in one significant way. Every household that came down with cholera derived water from the same source—the Broad Street well. Neighbors may or may not have been sick, but everyone who got their water from the Broad Street well was getting sick with cholera. Their water source was contaminated. Snow convinced the City Health Board to remove the pump handle from the Broad Street well and the epidemic stopped. Crisis averted.

> Social Media doesn't create heart
> sickness; it just reveals it.

Our heart is a source. The Bible likens it to a well. But if that well has been contaminated, every drop of water that comes from it will create symptoms of illness. In the Broad Street well case, everyone recognized the symptoms, but it took John Snow to identify the source. And just like the people of London, we are prone to blame everything but the true source of our problems. Social media is not the issue; our hearts are the issue. We need someone to cleanse the well.

Guard the Well

When our life is united to Christ's by faith, we are united to a fountain that never runs dry. If we would but drink from the fountain of living water rather than attempt to dig our own wells, we would experience the life God intends for us.

God diagnoses our hearts and tells they are sick, not because He hates us, but because He loves us. God's uncovering of our true condition is an act of great love and mercy. He longs to heal us.

God Himself is the fountain of living water (Jer. 2:13). The gospel is an abundant offer of grace and freedom that comes to us as Jesus takes the throne of our hearts and gives us "water welling up into eternal life" (John 4:14). This regeneration and ongoing renewal of our hearts happens as all lesser affections dry up and worship for God flows in. As Augustine says, "Thou hast made us for thyself, and our hearts won't rest until they find rest in you."[1]

A restless heart is a diseased heart—a heart that's been drinking from a contaminated well. This restlessness can be diagnosed like any other disease—by looking at the symptoms. What we consider social media "drawbacks" or "pitfalls" are really symptoms of heart sickness. But we can't manage or medicate ourselves out of these symptoms; we must be healed from them. God offers us this healing by giving us a new heart when we put our faith in Jesus: "And I will give you a new heart, and a new spirit I will put within you. And I will remove the heart of stone from your flesh and give you a heart of flesh" (Ezek. 36:26).

Here, God adds another layer to the well analogy. He tells us our hearts are like stone without Him—callous and unfeeling. Because our hearts have become numb, we look for things to make us feel alive and wanted and loved and free. We give ourselves over to things we hope will satisfy our desires for a time.

This is true even after He has given us new hearts. We still have a tendency to become hardhearted. We still have a tendency to try to satisfy our thirst by drinking from broken wells. So we still need the gospel to refresh and renew us time and time again. We still need the living water Jesus offers. It's not a one-time visit to this life-giving fountain that we need, but frequent, regular visits. That's what abiding in Christ looks like. Thankfully, it's not all up to us to stay connected to Jesus. The Holy Spirit is the "living water" Jesus was referring to, and He lives inside of us, guiding us, comforting us, and pointing us back to Jesus.

> We long for love, approval, joy, pleasure, justification, companionship, community, hope, and more, and we use social media as a tool to make our numb hearts feel alive again.

All of social media's drawbacks exist because we want to feel something in our hearts. We long for love, approval, joy, pleasure, justification, companionship, community, hope, and more, and we use social media as a tool to make our numb hearts feel alive again.

But, again, these substitutes are never enough. So God gives us a new heart of flesh that trusts Jesus. In Him, we are alive, wanted, loved, and free. We are given a new community, real companionship, and joy that isn't fleeting. In Jesus, we have ultimate approval from God our Father; we don't have to try to justify ourselves or our opinions on social media because we have already been completely justified by Jesus.

Of course, it's a battle to believe these things and to live out of the truth of who we are in Jesus. Our hearts are still prone to wander. The old hymn, "Come Thou Fount," describes our struggle:

Come though fount of every blessing,
Tune my heart to sing they grace,
streams of mercy never ceasing,
call for songs of loudest praise.

And then the last verse says:

O to grace how great a debtor, daily I'm constrained to be,
Let thy goodness like a fetter, bind my wandering heart
to thee.
Prone to wander Lord I feel it, prone to leave the God
I love.
Here's my heart Lord, take and seal it, seal it for thy
courts above.

From the first verse to the final verse we can see the trajectory of even a redeemed heart. Upon conversion, we sing the praises of our God, from whom all blessings flow. He is a fountain of mercy streaming into our hearts, creating songs of resounding praise. Yet, over time, our hearts are prone to wander from the God we love.

This wandering occurs when we fail to guard the well of our hearts. Our father Adam had the opportunity to guard the well of his heart, and He failed. The serpent slithered in and poisoned the well, causing Adam to doubt what God had told him. Like Adam before us, each of us is called to guard the well of hearts, but also like Adam, we simply can't do it on our own.

The gospel reminds us that Jesus did for us what we can't do for ourselves, such as we are, tempted by sin, weak and insufficient. Not only did Jesus guard the well and do the impossible for us, but also He died and rose to give us a brand-new well to drink from—a well springing up into eternal life (John 4:14).

When we trust Jesus, we are given a new heart with new desires and new affections. Understanding our new reality is the key to understanding how lasting change occurs. Every day, by faith and the power of the Holy Spirit, we are able to renounce the desires of the old heart and lean into the desires of the new one.

We do not guard our hearts by simply trying harder to do better. We cannot guard the well by creating a social media checklist to live by. Checklists can be helpful, but they aren't enough. It isn't enough to outline all of the potential pitfalls that social media offers. Addressing the symptoms and neglecting the cause is like constantly walking around with tissues but never taking medicine to help cure the illness. Sure, the tissues help, but they aren't a permanent solution. Lists, boundaries, and discipline may be temporarily helpful for managing symptoms, but we need a physician to heal our sickness.

In Christ, we guard our hearts by submitting ourselves to the God of mercy. We acknowledge our propensity to wander from the Source, and we run to the fountain of grace, asking Him to give us the living water we desperately need. It's the goodness of God that binds our hearts to Christ. It's God's kindness that leads to repentance (Rom. 2:4). No amount of self-discipline or focused intention can accomplish what Christ has already accomplished on our behalf. Therefore, guarding the well ultimately means *being guarded* by the well.

In the Gospels, Jesus uses different metaphors to explain His person and work. In John 10, He is the door to the sheepfold and also the shepherd of the sheep. In the Book of

Hebrews, He is the High Priest who offers the sacrifice and also the sacrifice itself.

> No amount of self-discipline or focused intention can accomplish what Christ has already accomplished on our behalf.

Similarly, Jesus is the One who guards the well, and also the source of the well itself. We guard the well by setting Christ apart in our hearts by faith. We reserve for Him the worship that He alone deserves.

The Symptoms	Our Shortcomings	Christ's Accomplishment
Time	We fail to steward our time in a way that honors God.	Christ spent every moment on earth intentionally fulfilling the Father's plan.
Speech	We often say what we shouldn't and refrain from saying what we should.	Christ only said what the Father gave Him to say.
Silence	We avoid silence and prefer to be distracted from true spiritual realities.	Christ often spent time alone in prayer, and He still intercedes for us at the Father's right hand.

The Symptoms	Our Shortcomings	Christ's Accomplishment
Self	We love ourselves in an unhealthy way.	Christ's love flowed outward to God and people. Self-denial and service marked His life and ministry.
People	We fail to love others and value them as God does.	Christ loved others with the perfect love of the Father.
Glory	We try to satisfy our hunger for glory by receiving it from human beings.	Christ received glory from God alone and was satisfied in Him.

Reflection Questions

Do you find your heart resting in the finished work of Christ? Or, do you search for substitutes to try to satisfy your longings?

Have you applied the gospel to your sin and shortcomings?

Is there anyone in your life who knows you well enough to know when you're restless and prone to wander? Do they have permission to discuss it with you?

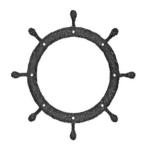

EPILOGUE:
PORT & ANCHOR

There really aren't simple answers for how to navigate the digital wave that's swept us up. So in some ways, we end up close to where we began—faced with a challenge. Waves of technology continue to lap up against the side of our vessel. How we proceed is up to us.

One thing is certain: we can't afford to turn back. The journey before us is of the Lord's choosing. He has determined when and where we should live (Acts 17:26). It was no surprise to Him that we would live in these days of incredible technological advancement. We have the opportunity to spread the gospel faster and wider than ever before, but as we've seen, there are challenges that go along with that. Amid all the change, we can be confident that our times are in His hands.

Still, my first tendency is to head back to shore when the waves begin to crash around the boat. I understand a bit more about how the disciples felt when they fearfully cried out for Jesus to save them from the storm (Matt. 8:25). There's this inward pull that causes me to want to simply wash my hands of these things altogether and not concern myself with them at all.

Sometimes the waves are so large and the clouds are so dark that our little boat is in danger of taking on water. In those times, I think it's OK to find a port to dock in until the storm passes. In other words, taking a break from social media is not the same as turning away from it for good.

A port is a place of refuge where we can resupply our vision and chart a new course. A port in the storm is a necessary haven for the navigator of the digital sea. Not everyone needs a year like me, but everyone needs a safe haven to rest in. Everyone needs some time to sit silently before God and relearn what it means to be connected, be in relationship, and to be loved by God.

And this is the key. Not all ports are created equally. Many of us have taken time to chart a new course for our digital lives, only to find ourselves heading right back in the same direction. We need both rest and guidance.

The gospel is our port in the storm, pointing us to Christ, who is our anchor, our compass, and our North Star on the journey. The gospel replenishes us, recalibrates us, and gives us refuge all at once. We find rest in the gospel that we could not find anywhere else, but we also find hope for the future there. We know we can't stay on land forever, and we don't want to.

Christ's voice calls us out upon uncertain, tumultuous waters to trust in His guiding hand.

The story of Christ calling Peter to walk on the water has always been so faith-building to me. We tend to forget that the winds of the storm were whipping against not only Peter but Jesus too. The boat was being rocked, the disciples were fearing for their lives, but Jesus didn't panic. He was in complete control. He was able to calm the storm.

Our faith needs to be anchored in Jesus, or we can easily be swept away by the storms of life. Even a "storm" as small as social media can cause us to sink unless Jesus upholds us.

Take time to rest in the truth of the gospel. Remind yourself of the eternal hope you have in Jesus. Let Him be the steady anchor that keeps you from sinking and the hopeful voice that bids you to keep sailing.

ACKNOWLEDGMENTS

To my wife, thank you for always faithfully encouraging me in the work of gospel ministry. If it weren't for you, this project would have never gained any traction at all. Thank you for listening to me as I read you these chapters over and over again. Most of all, thank you for reflecting the love of Jesus to me on a daily basis. You are a lily among the brambles. You are my best friend and I love you dearly.

To Providence Community Church, I thank God often for the gift that you all are to me. There truly is great joy in seeing you grow in the grace and knowledge of the Lord Jesus. The heart of this book flows from a heart for you all. Here is to many more years of making the gospel unignorable together!

To the elders at Providence, thank you for your brotherhood, constant support, and gospel encouragement. Nothing can replace brothers in arms. Thank you for being models of consistency and faithfulness—pillars of clay strengthened by the Cornerstone.

To David Lopez, thank you for your research and willingness to use your gifts for this project. Your labor helped shape this book.

To the team at Lucid Books, thank you for a wonderful experience getting this resource into more hands to serve more people. Your professionalism, skill, and personal touch made this book exponentially better than I could have hoped.

Finally and most importantly, glory to Christ who rescued me from drowning in a sinful sea of my own making. Soli Deo Gloria.

ENDNOTES

Introduction

1. Justin Wise, *The Social Church: A Theology of Digital Communication* (Chicago: Moody Publishers, 2014), 104–105.

2. Ed Stetzer, "How Should We Engage Culture," *Christianity Today,* April 16, 2010, http://www.christianitytoday.com/edstetzer/2010/april/how-should-we-engage-culture.html.

Chapter One

1. William Powers, *Hamlet's Blackberry: A Practical Philosophy for Building a Good Life in the Digital Age* (New York: HarperCollins, 2010), https://books.google.com/books?id=jQzwOpq1UMwC&printsec=frontcover&source=gbs_ge_summary_r&cad=0#v=onepage&q&f=false.

2. Ibid.

3. Dave Eggers, *The Circle* (New York: Vintage Books, 2013), https://books.google.com/books?id=sbxWAAAAQBAJ&printsec=frontcover&dq=the+circle+dave+eggers&hl=en&sa=X&ved=0ahUKEwjvoaapyffPAhWr7oMKHa1gDskQ6wEIKDAA#v=onepage&q=in%20a%20moment%20of%20sudden%20clarity&f=false.

Chapter Two

1. Arie Amaya-Akkermans, "The Story of Reconciliation," http://www.hannaharendtcenter.org/the-story-of-reconciliation/.

2. *Adults' Media Use and Attitudes: Report 2016*, accessed April 23, 2016, https://www.ofcom.org.uk/__data/assets/pdf_file/0026/80828/2016-adults-media-use-and-attitudes.pdf.

3. Keith Wilcox, quoted in Elizabeth Bernstein, "Why Are We So Rude Online," *The Wall Street Journal*, http://www.wsj.com/articles/SB100008723963904445924045780303 51784405148.

4. Joel Stein, "How Trolls Are Ruining the Internet," *Time*, August 18, 2016, http://time.com/4457110/internet-trolls/.

5. Andrew Sullivan, "I Used To Be a Human Being," *New York*, September 18, 2016, http://nymag.com/selectall/2016/09/andrew-sullivan-technology-almost-killed-me.html.

6. Ibid.

7. Ibid.

8. Robert Putnam, *Bowling Alone: The Collapse and Revival of American Community* (New York: Simon & Schuster Paperbacks, 2000), https://books.google.com/books ?id= rd2ibodep7UC&printsec=frontcover&dq=bowling +alone&hl=en&sa=X&ved=0ahUKEwik9P-kyvfPAhWI6 YMKHQhUCl0Q6AEIHjAA#v=onepage&q=Social%20 capital%20may%20turn%20out%20to%20be%20a%20 prerequisite%20for&f=false, 177.

9. Justin Wise, *The Social Church*, 154–160.

10. Ibid., 154–155.

11. Hui-Tzu Grace Chou and Nicholas Edge, "Cyberpsychology, Behavior, and Social Networking," February 2012, 15 (2): 117–121, doi: 10.1089/cyber.2011.0324.

12. Ibid.

13. Ibid.

14. Bruce Feiler, "For the Love of Being Liked," *New York Times*, May 9, 2014, http://www.nytimes.com/2014/05/11/ fashion/for-some-social-media-users-an-anxiety-from-approval-seeking.html?_r=0.

15. Ibid.

Chapter Three

1. Momar Vitaya, "How a Facebook Status Changed Jay Jaboneta's Life," *Asian Journal*, April 16, 2014, http:// asianjournal.com/aj-magazines/how-a-facebook-status-changed-jay-jabonetas-life/; See also, Facebook Stories

http://www.facebookstories.com/stories/3784/beyond-the-yellow-boat.

2. Ibid.

3. Ibid.

4. "How One Stupid Tweet Blew Up Justine Sacco's Life," *New York Times*, February 12, 2015, http://www.nytimes.com/2015/02/15/magazine/how-one-stupid-tweet-ruined-justine-saccos-life.html.

5. Ibid.

6. Ibid.

7. Ibid.

8. Devon Murphy, "Amanda Todd: Bullied to Death" *Huffington Post*, October 12, 2012, http://www.huffington post.ca/devon-murphy/amanda-todd_b_1961562.html.

9. https://www.youtube.com/watch?v=vOHXGNx-E7E.

Chapter Four

1. James A. Dewar, "The Information Age and the Printing Press Looking Back to Look Ahead," *Ubiquity*, August 31, 2000, http://ubiquity.acm.org/article.cfm?id=348784.

2. Charles Spurgeon, WikiQuote, accessed October 24, 2016, https://en.wikiquote.org/wiki/Charles_Spurgeon.

3. Elisabeth Elliot, *The Journals of Jim Elliot* (Grand Rapids: Baker Publishing Group, 1978).

Chapter Five

1. Tim Keller, "Deconstructing Defeater Beliefs: Leading the Secular to Christ," http://www.newcityindy.org/wp-con tent/uploads/2011/07/Deconstructing-Defeater-Beliefs. Tim-Keller.pdf.

2. Keller, quoted in Erik Raymond, "Keller: You Never Get Beyond the Gospel," September 9, 2009, https://blogs. thegospelcoalition.org/erikraymond/2009/09/09/keller-you-never-get-beyond-the-gospel/.

Chapter Six

1. Nikki Daniel, "Facebook, Moms, and the Last Day," *Gospel Coalition*, February 20, 2015, https://www.thegospel coalition.org/article/facebook-moms-and-the-last-day.

2. Ursula K. Le Guin, *A Wizard of Earthsea* (Boston: Houghton Mifflin Harcourt Publishing, 1968), https:// books.google.com/books?id=hDtjOj5FL8MC&print sec=frontcover&source=gbs_ge_summary_r&cad=0#v= onepage&q&f=false.

3. Richard Curtis, *About Time* (Universal Studios Home Entertainment, 2014), DVD.

4. Ibid.

Chapter Eight

1. Jacob Olesen, "Fear of Silence Phobia—Sedatephobia," http://www.fearof.net/fear-of-silence-phobia-sedate phobia/.

2. Sullivan, "I Used To Be a Human Being."

3. Charles Spurgeon, "Morning and Evening—October 12," Teaching the Word Ministries, http://www.teaching theword.org/apps/articles/default.asp?blogid=5771 &view=post&articleid=59834.

4. Oliver Burkeman, "This Column Will Change Your Life: Just Sit Down and Think," *The Guardian*, July 19, 2014, https://www.theguardian.com/lifeandstyle/2014/jul/19/ change-your-life-sit-down-and-think.

Chapter Nine

1. Kelly M. Kapic and Justin Taylor, *Communion with the Triune God* (Wheaton, IL.: Crossway, 2007), https://books.google. com/books?id=cKNbBAAAQBAJ&printsec=frontcover &source=gbs_ge_summary_r&cad=0#v=onepage& q&f=false.

2. Lewis, *Mere Christianity.*

3. Ibid.

Chapter Ten

1. C.S. Lewis, *The Weight of Glory and Other Addresses* (New York: Harper Collins Publishing, 1976), https://books .google.com/books?id=WNTT_8NW_qwC&printsec= frontcover&dq=The+Weight+of+Glory+and+Other +Addresses&hl=en&sa=X&ved=0ahUKEwjpi-P49vvPAh UJ7oMKHVc8ApEQ6AEIHjAA#v=onepage&q=The%20 Weight%20of%20Glory%20and%20Other%20Addresses &f=false.

Chapter Eleven

1. Ann Oldenburg, "Olympic Arrogance vs. Olympic Humility," *Lifezette*, August 11, 2016, http://www.lifezette.com/ popzette/olympic-arrogance-vs-olympic-humility/.

2. C.S. Lewis, *The Weight of Glory.*

3. Ibid.

Chapter Twelve

1. Augustine of Hippo, *The Confessions of St. Augustine* (New York: Doubleday Religion, 1960).